TESTIMONY ON U.S. POLICY TOWARDS IRAQ AND SYRIA AND THE THREAT POSED BY THE ISLAMIC STATE OF IRAQ AND THE LEVANT (ISIL)

TUESDAY, SEPTEMBER 16, 2014

U.S. SENATE,
COMMITTEE ON ARMED SERVICES,
Washington, DC.

The committee met, pursuant to notice, at 9:36 a.m. in room SH–216, Hart Senate Office Building, Senator Carl Levin (chairman) presiding.

Committee members present: Senators Levin, Reed, Nelson, McCaskill, Udall, Hagan, Manchin, Shaheen, Gillibrand, Blumenthal, Donnelly, Hirono, Kaine, King, Inhofe, McCain, Sessions, Wicker, Ayotte, Fischer, Graham, Vitter, and Lee.

Committee staff members present: Peter K. Levine, staff director; Travis E. Smith, chief clerk; and Leah C. Brewer, nominations and hearings clerk.

Majority staff members present: Creighton Greene, professional staff member; Michael J. Kuiken, professional staff member; Mariah K. McNamara, special assistant to the staff director; William G.P. Monahan, counsel; and Michael J. Noblet, professional staff member.

Minority staff members present: John A. Bonsell, minority staff director; Adam J. Barker, professional staff member; Steven M. Barney, minority counsel; Thomas W. Goffus, professional staff member; Daniel A. Lerner, professional staff member; Gregory R. Lilly, minority clerk; and Natalie M. Nicolas, minority research analyst.

Staff assistants present: Daniel J. Harder, Brendan J. Sawyer, and Alexandra M. Hathaway.

Committee members' assistants present: Carolyn A. Chuhta, assistant to Senator Reed; Cathy Haverstock, assistant to Senator Nelson; Christopher M. Cannon, assistant to Senator Hagan; C. Patrick Hayes and Paul C. Hutton IV, assistants to Senator Manchin; Patrick T. Day, assistant to Senator Shaheen; Moran Banai, assistant to Senator Gillibrand; Ethan A. Saxon, assistant to Senator Blumenthal; David J. Park, assistant to Senator Donnelly; Nick Ikeda, assistant to Senator Hirono; Karen E. Courington, assistant to Senator Kaine; Steven M. Smith, assistant to Senator King; Christian D. Brose, assistant to Senator McCain; Joseph G. Lai, assistant to Senator Wicker; Bradley L. Bowman, assistant to Senator Ayotte; Peter Schirtzinger, assistant to Senator Fisher; Craig R. Abele, assistant to Senator Graham; Joshua S. Hodges, assistant to Senator Vitter; Peter H. Blair, assistant to Senator Lee; and Victoria Coates, assistant to Senator Cruz.

OPENING STATEMENT OF SENATOR CARL LEVIN, CHAIRMAN

Chairman LEVIN. The committee will come to order. We're asking all the audience now to either take their seats and be quiet or please leave.

This morning, the committee receives testimony from the Secretary of Defense and the Chairman of the Joint Chiefs of Staff on the threat posed by the Islamic State of Iraq and the Levant, known as ISIS or ISIL, and on the President's strategy for addressing this threat.

Secretary Hagel and General Dempsey, we welcome you both. We look forward to your testimony.

ISIS has terrorized the Iraqi and Syrian people, engaging in kidnappings, killings, persecutions of religious minorities, and attacking schools, hospitals, and cultural sites. ISIS has brought home its barbarity with the brutal beheading of American journalists, James Foley and Steven Sotloff, and British aid worker, David Haines.

While ISIS is currently focused on building an Islamic caliphate in the Middle East, its poisonous ideology is hostile, not only to the region, but to the world, and there is real risk that the area it controls could become a launching pad for future terrorist attacks against the United States and our allies. This threat is amplified by foreign fighters who travel from Western countries to join with ISIS and then return to their countries of origin with advanced training and fighting experience.

I recently returned from Iraq, where U.S. airstrikes are helping Kurdish Peshmerga forces and Iraqi Security Forces break ISIS's momentum. However, our military leaders and intelligence experts uniformly say that airstrikes alone will not be sufficient to defeat ISIS. A number of elements of a successful strategy against ISIS are embodied in the approach outlined by the President last week.

First, the participation of key Arab states in the region will be critical to the effectiveness of any international coalition. If Western countries act in Iraq and Syria without visible participation and leadership of Arab nations, it will play into the propaganda pitch of the violent extremists that we are interested in dominating Iraq and Syria. ISIS's poisonous strand of Islam is a threat to all Muslim countries and can only be purged in a lasting way by mainstream Islam in the Arab world.

The international conferences in Jeddah last week and in Paris yesterday were a good start, with a number of Arab states declaring their shared commitment to develop a strategy, "to destroy ISIL wherever it is, including in both Iraq and Syria," and joining in an international pledge to use, "whatever means necessary," to achieve this goal.

Second, our assistance has been requested by the Government of Iraq, which has made a commitment to govern in an inclusive manner. The effort to rid Iraq of ISIS cannot be successful without the support of all elements of Iraqi society, including not only Shi'ites, Kurds, and religious minorities, but also the Sunni tribes, who strongly oppose the Maliki Government. The more the new government in Baghdad does to address the grievances of Iraq's Sunni communities, the more successful they will be in helping rid their country and the world of the ISIS poison.

Third, the President has announced that combat operations in Iraq and Syria will be carried out by Iraqis and Syrians with the support of a broad international coalition. That is the better approach, because, in this part of the world, the use of military force by Western nations can be counterproductive if it is not done correctly. In the absence of a Western target on the ground, ISIS's actions will undermine its own cause, because its brutality will continue to be targeted at fellow Muslims. We should be fully engaged in training and equipping Iraqis, Syrians, Kurds, and other local forces that are willing to take on ISIS, but we should try to counter the narrative of fanatics who attack Western combat forces on the ground as an occupation.

I believe the President, under both domestic and international law, has the authority to conduct the type of limited military campaign that he outlined last week. However, bipartisan, bicameral congressional support will make it easier for the President to build an international coalition, including the open and visible support of Arab countries. We should have the chance, before we leave, to vote on legislation that would authorize the U.S. military to openly train and equip the vetted moderate opposition in Syria, and I hope that Congress can come together to support it.

Senator Inhofe.

STATEMENT OF SENATOR JAMES M. INHOFE

Senator INHOFE. Thank you, Mr. Chairman.

After a year of the White House indecision and handwringing, the President finally presented to the American people his strategy to defeat ISIS. However, that was announced last week, fell short in two vital areas that I want to share with you:

First, the President again failed to acknowledge the seriousness of the threat that ISIS poses to the U.S. national security in its homeland. His claim that America is safer may support his political narrative, but it's not true.

Secretary Hagel, I appreciate your honesty when you described ISIS, on August the 21st, and you said that it's a imminent threat to every interest we have, whether it's in Iraq or anyplace else. I agree with you. ISIS has reported 35,000 fighters, nearly three times larger than it was in June. It's tripled since June and is growing larger every day. It's estimated that at least 2,000 fighters hold Western passports and at least 100 are U.S. citizens. This, coupled with their vast resources, large safe haven, blood, thirst to kill more Americans, is a recipe for disaster. The administration continues to say, "No specific evidence of plots against the homeland exist." Now, I want to remind everyone that we didn't have any specific evidence of plots against the homeland before September 11.

Now we face an extremist organization that is larger, more brutal, better networked, and better funded than al Qaeda ever was. I believe it's critical to have in the record the—that we establish today—how ISIS is fundamentally different from al Qaeda.

First of all, al Qaeda hides in caves. ISIS takes holds of governments' territories the size of my State of Oklahoma.

Second, al Qaeda has small groups of specialized fighters using terrorist tactics. ISIS is an army, with tanks, artillery, using conventional military, insurgent, and terrorist tactics.

Al Qaeda is based in remote religions—regions of the world. ISIS sits in—on Europe's doorstep.

Al Qaeda outdated propaganda on—has—uses the outdated propaganda and Arab-language media, but ISIS uses sophisticated media in multiple languages, including English, to spread its cause to recruit fighters.

Al Qaeda spent $1 million—this is very significant, Mr. President—Mr. Chairman—they spent $1 million on September 11. ISIS, we were going to say, until today, takes more than $1 million every day. There is an AP story this morning that shows, very convincingly, that they have access to an additional $3 million every day.

Now, the second thing that I think is of—a vital area. The President's strategy to defeat ISIS is fundamentally detached from the reality on the ground. Let's be clear. ISIS commands a territory—a terrorist army comprised of tens of thousands of organized fighters who have tanks, antitank missiles, and artillery. Its conventional battlefield successes have allowed it to triple its ranks in size in only 3 months. It will take an army to beat an army. But, instead, the President presented the limited counterterrorism strategy that he compared to his approach in Yemen and Somalia. The difference between al Qaeda in Yemen and Somalia and that of ISIS are enormous, and our strategy for each should reflect that reality. Taking this one-size-fits-all is a—destined for failure.

General Deptula, architect of the successful U.S. air campaign that destroyed the Taliban army on the battlefield in 2001, said—and this is a quote—he said, "We need to institute an aggressive air campaign in which air power is applied like a thunderstorm, not like a drizzle." Furthermore, airstrikes can only be fully effective, especially in urban areas in—ISIS is entrenched in, when paired with skills of a trained air controller on the ground. The President—but, the President already ruled out boots on the ground. There was a collective sigh of relief at ISIS headquarters in Syria when they heard him say that. His claim of "no boots on the ground" is an insult to the men and women in Iraq today who are serving in harm's way. We already have boots on the ground, in Erbil, in Baghdad, and throughout Iraq. We should ask the pilots dropping bombs over Iraq whether they think they are in combat, pilots who have faced the real threat of having to eject over ISIS-held territory. I am not advocating an army division or combat elements on the ground, but it is foolhardy for the Obama administration to tie the hands and so firmly rule out the possibility of air controllers and special operators on the ground to direct airstrikes and advise fighter forces. It sends the wrong message to our troops, to the enemy, and to partners.

And furthermore, if Congress does authorize the training and equipping of the Syrian moderate opposition, and then pushes them into combat without advisors on the ground, that effort is most likely to fail.

And we still don't have the answers to the most important and fundamental questions about what we're ultimately trying to accomplish, such as, What does a defeated or destroyed ISIS look like?

Finally, I hope we get the answers today, not only to the President's strategy, but also about the current state of our military residents. General Dempsey, nothing significant has changed, but when you warned, on February 12th of last year, not this year, that our military's on a path where the force may become, quote, "so degraded and so unready that it would be immoral to use force," unquote—when 6 years of massive budget cuts and another round of defense sequestration is on the horizon, we are still on that path. Despite this, the administration is still calling on our military to support its pivot to Asia, bolster our European allies against a growing Russian threat, successfully transition our missions in Afghanistan, support the response to the ebola—and, by the way, we hear, this morning, another 3,000 troops are going to be going over there—and now to launch a—military operations against ISIS in Iraq and Syria—unlike what the President seems to believe, you can't have it both ways. You can't slash our Defense budget, on one hand, while expecting our military to do it, on the other. If we want our military men and women to go into harm's way and defend this country, we need to give them the training, the tools, and the support they need to succeed. Without a ready, capable military, the President's imperfect strategy will remain what has become the trademark of this administration: a lot of tough talk that isn't backed by meaningful action.

I was hoping we could debate these broadly important issues with the NDAA, but we have not been able to do that, so it looks like, Mr. Chairman, that this is it.

Thank you.

Chairman LEVIN. Thank you, Senator Inhofe.

Secretary Hagel.

STATEMENT OF HON. CHARLES T. HAGEL, SECRETARY OF DEFENSE

Secretary HAGEL. Chairman Levin, Senator Inhofe, members of the committee, Chairman Dempsey and I very much appreciate the opportunity——

Chairman LEVIN. Okay, would you—we're asking you again to please sit down, and, if not, we're going to ask you to leave. No, thank you—thank you for—would you please now leave? Would you please now leave? I am asking you to please leave. You're acting very warlike, yourself. Would you please leave?

Thank you.

Secretary Hagel.

Secretary HAGEL. Mr. Chairman, as I was saying, Chairman Dempsey and I very much appreciate the opportunity this morning to discuss the President's strategy to degrade and ultimately defeat ISIL.

As you know—you all know—today, President Obama is in Atlanta, meeting with CDC officials regarding the ebola crisis, and then will travel tonight to Tampa to receive a briefing from the Commander of U.S. Central Command, General Austin, on operational plans to implement his ISIL strategy. I'll join the President tomorrow in Tampa for that briefing.

The Defense Department's civilian and military leaders are in complete agreement that the United States and our allies and partners must take action against ISIL and that the President's strategy is the right approach. However, as President Obama has repeatedly made clear, American military power alone cannot—will not eradicate the threats posed by ISIL to the United States, our allies, and our friends and partners in the region. Iraq's continued political progress toward a more inclusive and representative government and its programs of reform and reconciliation will be critical to achieve the progress required. We believe that new Iraqi Minister—Prime Minister Abadi is committed to bringing all Iraqis together against ISIL. To support him and the Iraqi people in their fight, the coalition will need to use all its instruments of power. We intend to use all of those instruments of power—military, law enforcement, economic, diplomatic, and intelligence—in coordination with all the countries in the region.

To succeed, this strategy will also require a strong partnership between our executive branch and our Congress. The President has made it a priority to consult with congressional leadership on the ISIL challenge, as have Vice President Biden, Secretary Kerry, and many senior members of the administration. I have appreciated the opportunities I have had to discuss the President's strategy with many members of this committee and other members of the Senate and the House over the last couple of weeks. We will continue to consult closely with Congress as this campaign moves forward.

ISIL poses a real threat to all countries in the Middle East, our European allies, and to America. In the last few months, the world has seen ISIL's barbarity up close as its fighters advanced across western and northern Iraq and slaughtered thousands of innocent civilians, including Sunni and Shi'a Muslims and Kurdish Iraqis in religious minorities. ISIL's murder of two U.S. journalists outraged the American people and exposed to the world the depravity of ISIL's ideology and tactics. Over the weekend, we saw ISIL's murder of a British citizen.

ISIL now controls a vast swath of eastern Syria and western and northern Iraq, including towns and cities in all of these areas. ISIL has gained strength by exploiting the civil war in Syria and sectarian strife in Iraq, and it has seized territory across both countries and acquired significant resources and advanced weapons. ISIL has employed a violent combination of terrorists, insurgent and conventional military tactics. ISIL has been very adept at developing technology in social media to increase its global profile and attract tens of thousands of fighters. Its goal is to become the new vanguard of a global extremist movement and establish an extremist Islamic caliphate across the Middle East. It considers itself the rightful inheritor of Osama bin Laden's legacy.

While ISIL clearly poses an immediate threat to American citizens in Iraq and our interests in the Middle East, we also know that thousands of foreign fighters, including Europeans and more than 100 Americans, have traveled to Syria with passports that give them relative freedom of movement. These fighters can exploit

ISIL's safe haven to plan, coordinate, and carry out attacks against the United States and Europe.

Although the intelligence community has not yet detected specific plotting against the U.S. homeland, ISIL has global aspirations. And, as President Obama has made clear, ISIL's leaders have threatened America and our allies. If left unchecked, ISIL will directly threaten our homeland and our allies.

In his address to the Nation last week, President Obama announced that the United States will lead a broad multinational coalition to roll back the ISIL threat. More than 40 nations have already expressed their willingness to participate in this effort, and more than 30 nations have indicated their readiness to offer military support. President Obama, Vice President Biden, Secretary Kerry, and I and others have been working, and will continue to work, to unite and expand this coalition.

At the NATO Summit in Wales, Secretary Kerry and I convened a meeting of key partners in the coalition. I then went to Georgia and Turkey. The Georgians made clear that they want to help. Turkey, by virtue of its geography and its common interest in destroying ISIL, which is holding 46 Turkish diplomats hostages, will play an important role—an important role in this effort. Turkey joined our meeting in Wales, and Secretary Kerry and I continue to discuss specific contributions Turkey will make.

Secretary Kerry convened a meeting in Jeddah last week with the foreign ministers from the six Gulf Corporation Councils, nations Egypt, Iraq, Jordan, and Lebanon, and all signed a communique to do their share in the comprehensive fight against ISIL, including joining in the many aspects of a coordinated military campaign against ISIL.

Also last week, 22 nations of the Arab League adopted a resolution at their summit in Cairo calling for comprehensive measures to combat ISIL.

And yesterday in Paris, French President Hollande, who traveled to Baghdad last weekend, hosted a conference attended by U.N. Security Council Permanent Members, European and Arab leaders, and representatives of the EU, Arab League, and United Nations. They all pledged to help Iraq in the fight against ISIL, including through military assistance.

Key allies, such as United Kingdom, France, and Australia, are already contributing military support, and other partners have begun to make specific offers.

At next week's U.N. General Assembly, we expect that additional nations will begin making commitments across the spectrum of capabilities, building on the strong Chapter 7 U.N. Security Council Resolution adopted last month, calling on all member states to take measures to counter ISIL and suppress the flow of foreign fighters to ISIL.

Also next week, President Obama will chair a meeting of the U.N. Security Council to further mobilize the international community. As you all know, former International Security Assistance Force Commander and Acting CENTCOM Commander, General John Allen, has been designated to serve as Special Presidential Envoy for the global coalition to counter ISIL. President Obama is meeting with General Allen this morning.

General Allen will work in a civilian diplomatic capacity to coordinate, build, and sustain the coalition, drawing on his extensive experience in the region. He will be the administration's point man to coordinate coalition contributions and to build support within the region. He will work closely with General Austin to ensure that coalition efforts are aligned across all elements of our strategy.

In his address to the Nation, the President outlined the four elements of this strategy to degrade and ultimately defeat ISIL. Let me now describe how we are implementing this whole-of-government approach:

First, in close coordination with the new Iraqi government, we are broadening our air campaign to conduct systematic airstrikes against ISIL targets. To protect Americans threatened by ISIL's advances and to prevent humanitarian catastrophe, the U.S. military has already conducted more than 160 successful airstrikes, which have killed ISIL fighters, destroyed weapons and equipment, and enabled Iraqi and Kurdish forces to get back on the offensive and secure key territory and critical infrastructure, including the Mosul and Haditha dams. These actions have disrupted ISIL tactically and have helped buy time for the Iraqi government to begin forming an inclusive and broadbased governing coalition led by the new Prime Minister. That was one of President Obama's essential preconditions for taking further action against ISIL, because the Iraqi people—the Iraqi people must be united in their opposition against ISIL in order to defeat them. This will require a united and inclusive government. This is ultimately their fight.

The new broader air campaign will include strikes against all ISIL targets and enable the Iraqi Security Forces, including Kurdish forces, to continue to stay on the offensive and recapture territory from ISIL, and hold it. Because ISIL operates freely across the Iraqi/Syrian border and maintains a safe haven in Syria, our actions will not be restrained by a broader—by a border in name only. As the President said last week, "If you threaten America, you will find no safe haven."

The President of the United States has the constitutional and the statutory authority to use military force against ISIL in Syria as well as Iraq. And CENTCOM is refining and finalizing those plans, which General Austin will brief to the President tomorrow in Tampa. This plan includes targeted actions against ISIL safe havens in Syria, including its command and control, logistics capabilities, and infrastructure. General Dempsey and I have both reviewed and approved the CENTCOM plan.

The second element of the strategy is to increase our support for forces fighting ISIL on the ground, the Iraqi and Kurdish forces and the moderate Syrian opposition. To support Iraqi and Kurdish forces, the President announced, last week, that he would deploy an additional 475 American troops to Iraq. Part of that number includes approximately 150 advisors and support personnel to supplement forces already in Iraq, conducting assessments of the Iraqi Security Forces. This assessment mission is now transitioning to an advise-and-assist mission, with more than 15 teams embedding with Iraqi Security Forces at the headquarters level to provide strategic and operational advice and assistance. The rest of the additional 475 troops include 125 personnel to support intelligence, surveillance, and reconnaissance missions out of Erbil and 200 personnel to increase headquarters elements in both Baghdad and Erbil, helping us better coordinate military activities across Iraq.

By the time all these forces arrive, there will be approximately 1600 U.S. personnel in Iraq responding to the ISIL threat. But, as the President said last week, American forces will not have a combat mission. Instead, these advisors are supporting Iraqi and Kurdish forces and supporting the government's plan to stand up Iraqi national guard units to help Sunni communities defeat ISIL.

The best counterweights to ISIL are local forces and the people of the area. And, as you know, in June the President asked Congress for the necessary authority for DOD to train and equip moderate Syrian opposition forces, and $500 million to fund this program. We have now secured support from Saudi Arabia to host the training program for this mission. And Saudi Arabia has offered financial and other support, as well. The 500-million request the President made in June for this train-and-equip program reflects CENTCOM's estimate of the cost to train, equip, and resupply more than 5,000 opposition forces over one year. The package of assistance that we initially provide would consist of small arms, vehicles, and basic equipment, like communications, as well as tactical and strategic training.

As these forces prove their effectiveness on the battlefield, we would be prepared to provide increasingly sophisticated types of assistance to the most trusted commanders and capable forces. Because DOD does not currently have the authority to conduct a train-and-equip mission, the administration has asked Congress to provide the authority in the Continuing Resolution it is currently now considering. A rigorous vetting process will be critical to the success of this program. DOD will work closely with the State Department, the intelligence community, and our partners in the region to screen and vet the forces we train and equip. We will monitor them closely to ensure that weapons do not fall into the hands of radical elements of the opposition, ISIL, the Syrian regime, or other extremist groups. There will always be risk—there will always be risks in a program like this, but we believe that risk is justified by the imperative of destroying ISIL and the necessity of having capable partners on the ground in Syria.

As we pursue this program, the United States will continue to press for a political resolution to the Syrian conflict resulting in the end of the Assad regime. Assad has lost all legitimacy to govern and has created the conditions that allowed ISIL and other terrorist groups to gain ground and terrorize and slaughter the Syrian population. The United States will not coordinate or cooperate with the Assad regime. We will also continue to counter Assad through diplomatic and economic pressure.

The third element of the President's strategy is an all-inclusive approach to preventing attacks from ISIL against the homelands of the United States and our allies. In concert with our international partners, the United States will draw on intelligence, law enforcement, diplomatic, and economic tools to cut off ISIL's funding, improve our intelligence, strengthen homeland defense, and stem the flow of foreign fighters in and out of the region.

The Department of Justice and the Department of Homeland Security have launched an initiative to partner with local communities to counter extremist recruiting. And the Department of Treasury's Office of Terrorism and Financial Intelligence is working to disrupt ISIL's financing and expose their activities.

The final element of the President's strategy is to continue providing humanitarian assistance to innocent civilians displaced or threatened by ISIL. Alongside the Government of Iraq, the United Kingdom, Canada, Australia, and France, U.S. troops have already delivered lifesaving aid to thousands of threatened Iraqi civilians on Mount Sinjar and the Iraqi town of Amirli. In total, the U.S. military conducted 32 airdrops of food and supplies, providing over 818,000 pounds of aid, including nearly 50,000 gallons of water and nearly 122,000 Meals Ready to Eat in these operations. In addition to this assistance, last week the State Department announced an additional 48 million in aid for civilian organizations to meet the urgent needs of Iraqis displaced by ISIL. Our total humanitarian assistance to displaced Iraqis is now more than $186 million for fiscal year 2014.

The United States is also the single largest donor of humanitarian assistance for the millions of Syrians affected by the civil war. Last week, Secretary Kerry announced an additional 500 million in humanitarian assistance. Since the start of the Syrian conflict, the United States has now committed almost $3 billion in humanitarian assistance to those affected by the civil war.

All four elements of this strategy require a significant commitment of resources on the part of the United States and our coalition partners.

Mr. Chairman, I think everyone on this committee understands fully, this will not be an easy or a brief effort. It is complicated. We are at war with ISIL, as we are with al-Qaeda. But, destroying ISIL will require more than military efforts alone, it will require political progress in the region and effective partners on the ground in Iraq and Syria. As the Congress and the administration work together, we know this effort will take time. The President has outlined a clear, comprehensive, and workable strategy to achieve our goals and protect our interests.

Mr. Chairman, Senator Inhofe, thank you for your continued support, and that of this committee, and your partnership.

Thank you.

[The prepared statement of Secretary Hagel follows:]

Chairman LEVIN. Thank you very much, Secretary Hagel.

Thank you. Would you please leave? Would you please leave the room now? We are asking you nicely, but—we are asking you nicely to please leave the room. Look, we are asking you nicely. Would you please leave the room? Thank you. We have asked you for the last time. Thank you very much. Thank you for leaving, and—thank you. Goodbye.

Now, General Dempsey, as soon as the noise is removed from the room.

We would ask all of you to avoid these kind of outbursts. They are not doing anybody any good, including hearing what this testimony is, and they are not doing you and whatever your cause is any good, either.

Thank you very much. Would you please—I am asking you nicely to please leave the room. We are asking you again. Would you please remove this gentleman? Thank you very much. Goodbye. Goodbye. Thank you.

General Dempsey.

STATEMENT OF GEN MARTIN E. DEMPSEY, USA, CHAIRMAN, JOINT CHIEFS OF STAFF

General DEMPSEY. Thank you, Chairman and Ranking Member Inhofe, members of the committee. I do appreciate the opportunity to appear before you this morning.

Secretary Hagel has described in detail the elements of our strategy against ISIL. The role the United States military is taking is, in my judgment, appropriate. This is an Iraq-first strategy, but not an Iraq-only one.

Job one is empowering the Iraqi ground forces to go on the offensive, which they are already beginning to demonstrate. This requires a partnership with a credible Iraqi government, which is also showing positive signs of becoming inclusive of all of its population.

Within this partnership, our advisors are intended to help the Iraqis develop a mindset for the offensive and to take actions consistent with offensive. Our military advisors will help the Iraqis conduct campaign planning, arrange for enabler and logistics support, and coordinate our coalition activities. If we reach the point where I believe our advisors should accompany Iraq troops on attacks against specific ISIL targets, I will recommend that to the President.

As long as ISIL enjoys a safe haven in Syria, it will remain a formidable force and a threat. So, while this work in Iraq is taking place, we will simultaneously pressure ISIL in Syria. With coalition partners and contributions, we will begin building a force of vetted, trained, moderate Syrians to take on ISIL in Syria. We will work to ensure that they have a Syrian chain of command and report to a moderate political authority. This force will work initially at the local and community level and help pull together Syrians who have most felt the harsh hand of ISIL.

In conjunction with that long-term effort, we will be prepared to strike ISIL targets in Syria that degrade ISIL's capabilities. This won't look like a "shock and awe" campaign, because that's simply not how ISIL is organized. But, it will be a persistent and sustainable campaign.

I want to emphasize that our military actions must be part of a whole-of-government effort that works to disrupt ISIL financing, interdict the movement of foreign fighters across borders, and undermine the ISIL message. Given a coalition of capable, willing regional and international partners, I believe we can destroy ISIL in Iraq, restore the Iran—correction—the Iraq/Syria border, and disrupt ISIL in Syria.

ISIL will ultimately be defeated when their cloak of religious legitimacy is stripped away and the population on which they have imposed themselves reject them. Our actions are intended to move in that direction. This will require a sustained effort over an extended period of time. It is a generational problem, and we should expect that our enemies will adapt their tactics as we adjust our approach.

As the situation in the Middle East evolves and continues to demand our attention, we are also balancing other challenges in other regions, ebola being the most recent, along with reassuring our European allies against Russian aggression and continuing our mission in Afghanistan. But, our young men and women in uniform are doing so much more. They conduct hundreds of exercises, activities, and engagements every day, actions that deter conflict and reassure allies around the world. They are performing magnificently.

But, I am growing increasingly uncomfortable that the will to provide means does not match the will to pursue ends. The Secretary and I are doing what we can inside the Department to bridge that gap, but we will need your help. If we do not depart from our present path, over time I will have fewer military options to offer to the Secretary and to the President, and that is not a position in which I want to find myself.

Thank you.

[The prepared statement of General Dempsey follows:]

[COMMITTEE INSERT]

Chairman LEVIN. Thank you very much, General Dempsey.

We are going to have a 6-minute first round. We have a lot of us here, and we all want to have an opportunity. And then, if we go around once and have a reasonable hour facing us, we will try to have a very short second round. But, we just won't know that until we get to it.

General Dempsey, let me start by asking you for your professional military opinion of the military strategy which was announced by the President last week. Do you personally support the strategy?

General DEMPSEY. I do, Mr. Chairman.

Chairman LEVIN. Can you tell us why?

General DEMPSEY. Because the nature of the threat is such that, as I mentioned, it will only be defeated when moderate Arab and Muslim populations in the region reject it. And therefore, the way forward seems to me to run clearly through a coalition of Arab and Muslim partners, and not through the ownership of the United States in this issue.

And so, the strategy does that. It seeks to build a coalition, encourage the—an inclusive government to address the grievances that have caused this in the first place. It applies military—U.S. military power where we have unique capability to do so. And over time, it allows those populations to reject ISIL.

Chairman LEVIN. And, in terms of utilizing the—on the ground, the forces that are Syrian and Iraqi rather than Western forces, is that part of the thinking at this time, as well, to avoid a Western ground force in a Arab or Muslim country, for the same reason that you just gave?

General DEMPSEY. Well, I do think that the approach to build a coalition and enable it leaves me to leverage our unique capabilities, which tend to be, as I mentioned, the ability to train and plan and provide intelligence and provide air power.

As I said in my statement, however, this—my view at this point is that this coalition is the appropriate way forward. I believe that will prove true. But, if it fails to be true, and if there are threats to the United States, then I, of course, would go back to the President and make a recommendation that may include the use of U.S. military ground forces.

Chairman LEVIN. Secretary Hagel, how important is it—and you've made reference to this, but I would like you to elaborate—that the coalition have very strong visible participation by Arab and Muslim states?

Secretary HAGEL. Mr. Chairman, you just reflected, in your question to General Dempsey, on the point, and I would pick up where General Dempsey left off. This is not a West-versus-East issue. This is not a U.S./European coalition against Muslim countries or a Muslim region. It's important that the world see, especially the people of the Middle East see, that the threat that is confronting them first, and all of us, needs to be addressed by the people of their region as well as all nations and all people in the world. To have Arab Muslim nations be present and public about their efforts in this coalition helps that. And it's critically important to the ultimate success of winning against all extremist factors and factions in the Middle East, specifically ISIL.

Chairman LEVIN. And that same approach of having the force—the people of these countries basically purge the strand of Islam that is so poisonous that is trying to take over in their countries, leads, I gather, to—is one argument for using indigenous national forces on the ground rather than outside, and particularly Western, forces.

Secretary HAGEL. Yes. I said in my statement, Mr. Chairman, that the most significant powerful force against extremism in the Middle East are the people, themselves, who will not accept this kind of barbarity and brutality. The Muslims of the world know that what ISIL represents in no way is what their religion, what their ethnicity, what their background represents. And to have the local forces be involved, supported by local people, is the most significant thing I think we can do as we support them, as we are doing and will continue to do in every way, to defeat ISIL and other extremist threats.

Chairman LEVIN. I believe that you have testified that the goal is to—on the equip and training of Syrian people—that the goal is to equip and train about 5,000 in 1 year. Now, how is that, first of all, going to match up against the ISIL numbers? And—well, let me just start with that one.

Secretary HAGEL. Well, as I have said, and the President said, and General Dempsey has said, and I think in our briefings here, in our closed session briefings we have had with members of the Senate and the House and our staff here last week—this week—5,000 is a beginning, Mr. Chairman. This is part of the reason this effort is going to be a long-term effort.

But, we will do it right. We will be able to train and equip these forces through our ability to give them tactical, give them strategic guidance in leadership, the kind of equipment they need, where they can move not just as bands of a few people, but as legitimate forces. Five thousand alone is not going to be able to turn the tide;

we recognize that on this side. On the ISIL side, on the different estimates that continue to come out, Mr. Chairman, because it is hard to pinpoint at any one time exactly what the strength of ISIL is. We know it's significant. We know, because of their successes over the last few months, they have picked up significant support. We also know that a lot of that support is forced support, "You will either be part of this or your families killed, or you will be killed." So, it is an imperfect process.

But, the 5,000 per year that—and we may do better; we might be able to do better than—but, we do not want to overstate or overpromise, because we want the right people, our part of the overall strategy that I articulated here, as outlined by the President.

Chairman LEVIN. Thank you very much.

Senator Inhofe.

Senator INHOFE. Thank you, Mr. Chairman.

I would ask that you turn the maps over. This is just for reference. We put this together, with the help of the military, with the help of some think tanks, and they—the colors represented there, the orange would be what is under ISIL control right now; the gray would be the Kurdish control; and then, the brown would be the ambitions of ISIL.

Do you look at that map and find any problem with it, either one of you? It's——

General DEMPSEY. Actually, Senator, in terms of their ambition, I think that is probably understating their ambition.

Senator INHOFE. Yes.

General DEMPSEY. I think, if left unaddressed, they would aspire to restore the ancient Kingdom of al-Sham, which includes the current state of Israel and runs all the way down to Kuwait. But, that's a——

Senator INHOFE. Yes, we are trying to be conservative on this——

General DEMPSEY. Yes.

Senator INHOFE.—but let people know, this is a big area, and it's a major——

Secretary Hagel, do you have a problem with this?

Secretary HAGEL. No. I think General Dempsey stated it exactly right.

Senator INHOFE. All right.

Okay. The—according to some of the reports, the U.S. intelligence agencies believe that ISIL does not represent the immediate threat to the United States. In fact, Daniel Benjamin, who was President Obama's top counterterrorism advisor during his first term, he said—and this is a quote—he said, "Members of the Cabinet and top military officers all over the place describing the threat in lurid terms that are just not justified."

And I appreciate, Secretary Hagel, the statement you made when you said that ISIS poses "an imminent threat to every interest we have, whether it's in Iraq or anyplace else." Do you still agree with that statement?

Secretary HAGEL. I do.

Senator INHOFE. Do you, General Dempsey?

General DEMPSEY. Yes, I do, Senator.

Senator INHOFE. You know, one of the things that I was glad to see is that the American people—there's been a wake-up call. Last week, there was a poll that was the—a CNN poll—that 70 percent of the people in America believe it's a threat to our homeland. Then yesterday, another one came out. This was a Wall Street Journal poll, the same thing, 70 percent of the people. So, I think that wake-up call has taken.

Now, when President Obama—and this gets back to some of the statements you made in your opening remarks—he said, "Our objective is clear. We will degrade and ultimately destroy ISIL through a comprehensive and sustained counterterrorism strategy." Now, it's clear—and we have talked about this side—this is an army. And I outlined, in my opening statement, the six basic differences between al-Qaeda and what we are facing right now. Do you generally agree with that?

General DEMPSEY. What I generally agree with, Senator, is that they have been using conventional tactics until such time as we applied air power, and that they're——

Senator INHOFE. So——

General DEMPSEY.—they're beginning to adapt now.

Senator INHOFE. So, now you don't agree that that strategy that we would impose against terrorists or some group is appropriate today with looking in terms of the giant army that we are facing.

General DEMPSEY. No, I agree we have to build the capability of the ISAF and the Pesh to address it conventionally——

Senator INHOFE. Okay.

General DEMPSEY.—while also including a counterterrorism component in our strategy.

Senator INHOFE. Okay.

Secretary Hagel, I would like to get in the record here as to who is in charge of the war, because we hear people like Ambassador Beecroft in the State Department that—saying that they are in a lot of the control. I—my—if it's CENTCOM Commander Austin, then I feel a lot better about it. Is that who is in control of this? It's now military?

Secretary HAGEL. Yes. As I said in my opening statement, Senator—I tried to frame some of that up in—for example, what I mentioned about General Allen's role, initial role, as a coordinating role. But, I also said that he would work directly in that coordination with General Austin as——

Senator INHOFE. Yes.

Secretary HAGEL.—as the CENTCOM Commander. That's why President Obama will be with the CENTCOM Commander in Tampa tomorrow to go over the plan.

Senator INHOFE. Sure. Sure.

Well, Mr. Secretary, I—my concern is, I don't want people to be under the delusion that this is just another effort—another terrorist effort that we are going to be pursuing.

Asked by a reporter on September 11th to define victory against ISIL, the White House Press Secretary said, "I didn't bring my Webster's Dictionary with me up here." Secretary Hagel, you didn't bring yours, either. Can you define what victory looks like to the United States——

Secretary HAGEL. When we——

Senator INHOFE.—against ISIL?

Secretary HAGEL. Well, I believe victory would be when we complete the mission of degrading and destroying, defeating ISIL, just as the President laid out that was his objective.

Senator INHOFE. Yes. Well, I understand that. That is not the—I got a different interpretation when I listened to his speech. When he said, on the fight against ISIL, quote, "It will not involve American combat troops fighting on the soil. American forces will not have a combat mission."

In your opinion—let me ask you two questions, General Dempsey—in your opinion, are the pilots dropping bombs in Iraq, as they're now doing, a direct combat mission? And, second, will U.S. forces be prepared to provide combat search and rescue if a pilot gets shot down, and will they put boots on the ground to make that rescue successful?

General DEMPSEY. Yes and yes.

Senator INHOFE. Good. Well, I appreciate that.

And then, the—lastly—the last question I have, because I know I have gone beyond my time. We have been complaining about what is happened in the funding, and then—now we are looking at the—at sequestration and all of this. In light of all of this that's occurred since we originally started talking about the funding that would be necessary, do you think we are adequately funded now to take care of all these things that we—I stated in my opening statement and you have also agreed to? Where are we on our funding? Are we adequate?

Secretary HAGEL. Well, two answers to your question. But, no is the first——

Senator INHOFE. Okay.

Secretary HAGEL.—basic answer. But, the budget that we will be coming up here presenting, as you know, in a few months, will contain what we believe is going to be required to carry forward, for the longer term, this effort. But, in the short term, this is why we are asking for the $500 million authority for the train and equip. Plus, as you know, the President had asked, a few months ago, for a $5 billion counterterrorism partnership fund, plus a billion-dollar European initiative fund, as well.

So, I think what General Dempsey said in his closing comments in his statement probably summarized pretty well. As you have noted, all of the different pressures that are now coming down on this country, residing, a good amount of it, at the Defense Department, one of the things that we have been warning about is sequestration over the last year and a half. So, we will come forward, in our budget for the next fiscal year, with some new requests.

Senator INHOFE. Okay. And——

General DEMPSEY. If I—could I just elaborate? On behalf of the Joint Chiefs, because we've discussed this frequently about our ability to balance capability, capacity, and readiness.

Last year, we said that we—the size of the force that was projected over the course of the POM, over the Future Year Defense Plan, was adequate to the task if the assumptions made were valid. And some of the assumptions we made were about commitments, and some of the assumptions we made were about our ability to get paid compensation, healthcare changes, infrastructure changes, and weapon systems. We didn't get any of those, actually, or very few of them, and the commitments have increased. So, this—we do have a problem, and it will—I think it'll become clear through the fall. And it's not a problem that we can solve just with OCO. That is to say, the operational contingency funds. There's a base budget issue here, too, we have to get at.

Senator INHOFE. I know that's true. I know that's true. But, you mentioned the Chiefs, and Odierno and the other Chiefs have come and testified in this room before us that, even before these things erupted, it was not adequate. As we all know, risk increases when the adequacy is not met.

Thank you, Mr. Chairman.

Chairman LEVIN. Thank you very much.

We have a quorum here now, and so I am going to ask the committee to consider the list of 2458 pending military nominations. They have been before the committee the required length of time. Is there a motion——

Senator INHOFE. I so move.

Chairman LEVIN.—to favorably report the nominations? Is there a second?

Senator REED. Second.

Chairman LEVIN. All in favor, say aye. [A chorus of ayes.]

Opposed, nay. [No response.]

The motion carries. Thank you very much.

Senator Reed.

Senator REED. Well, thank you, Mr. Chairman.

And, gentlemen, thank you for your testimony.

General Dempsey, we have had a debate going on and on about no boots on the ground, some boots on the ground, no boots on the ground. It might help us all if you would clarify precisely what our forces are doing in Iraq today. And you all suggested that if the situation changes, you might recommend or come to us with a recommendation that they would enhance their mission or change their mission. But, can you clarify what they are doing?

General DEMPSEY. Yes, I can. Thanks for asking, Senator.

The—first of all, I think everyone should be aware, when we talk about combat forces, we—that's all we grow. We—when we bring a young man or woman into the military, they come in to be a combat soldier or a combat marine or a combat—we don't bring them in to be anything other than combat-capable. But, that is different than how we use them. And, in the case of our contributions in Iraq right now, the airmen, as the chairman—as the ranking member mentioned, are very much in a combat role. The folks on the ground are in a—very much a combat advisory role. They are not participating in direct combat. There is no intention for them to do so. I have mentioned, though, that if I found that circumstance evolving, that I would, of course, change my recommendation.

An example. If the Iraqi Security Forces and the Pesh were at some point ready to retake Mosul, a mission that I would find to be extraordinarily complex, it could very well be part of that particular mission to provide close combat advising or accompanying for that mission. But, for the day-to-day activities that I anticipate will evolve over time, I don't see it to be necessary right now.

Senator REED. One of the presumptions—and I will just raise it—would be, because we are using air power, that there is sufficient capacity in the Iraqi forces to coordinate that air power on the ground? Is that sort of the issue you are looking at, or that is an issue——

General DEMPSEY. No, we have, Senator. And we have come—let me use the Mosul Dam operation as a great example of that. So, on the ground, we had the Peshmerga, and we had the counterterrorist service from the Iraqi Security Forces, and then, in a—an operation center in Erbil, we had our own folks, using predator feeds and a system we call the ROVER to be able to help the Iraqis manage the battle on the ground. Incredibly complex. Three languages: English, Kurdish, and Arab. And we worked through it. It was a real challenge, but we worked through it. And, as we did, we learned some things about how to use advisors from remote locations.

I am not saying this will work every place, every time. But, we pulled that mission off, and I think it's a good template for future operations.

Senator REED. And—but, I presume one of the areas you are really looking at is these capable Iraqis who can communicate and coordinate on the ground, their special forces particularly.

General DEMPSEY. Trained by us, that's right.

Senator REED. Right.

Mr. Secretary, we are—or, you are proposing, the President's proposing, to train about 5,000 individuals a year to go back into Syria. The Saudis have agreed to host it in some manner. How do you integrate these forces back into Syria? Will they go in as units? Will they—what's the plan after they are trained? Because I think that is part of the issue.

Secretary HAGEL. Senator, one of the points that I made a couple of minutes ago, in answering Senator Inhofe's question, was the point about training them as units so they can operate as units, which is—as you know, with your military experience, is critically important as you build an effective opposition force, not just a hit-and-run group of rebels, but an effective force—command-control, tactics, strategy. And so, yes, that is the fundamental training principle of how we begin.

The length of the time here depends on a number of things, but we are probably talking about 8 weeks per cycle. That might move, within a week or two. But, that's the intent of how they would train up.

The CENTCOM leaders are already focused on that, are already structured to do that, are preparing. And one of the things the President will get tomorrow, as he spends the day with General Austin and the CENTCOM planners and commanders in Tampa, is taking him through that entire structure.

Senator REED. Thank you.

General Dempsey, I think in your remarks, or the Secretary's remarks, you suggested that the immediate operations will probably most likely be in Iraq, simply because we have the Iraqi National Security Forces, we are already partnering them, we just conducted strike. But, that will put ISIL in the position of, as we hopefully become more effective, of making a decision to reinforce or to respond in Iraq and weaken them in Syria or to pull back into Syria. So, I think your strategy is probably the most effective use of what we have at the time, but would you like to comment on that?

General DEMPSEY. Well, the strategy is to squeeze ISIL from multiple directions so that they can't do what they have been doing, which is maneuver places where they're not under pressure. So, if we can get the Government of Iraq to reach out to these populations that have been disadvantaged during the Maliki regime so that the ISIL doesn't have a free-flowing stream in which to float, and if we can get the ISAF—and we have done an assessment of the 50 brigades of the ISAF around Baghdad, we know which ones are capable of partnering and improving their capabilities—if we can get enough of them to go on the offensive, both west and north, get the Peshmerga to squeeze from the—from north to south, and then find a way, over time, in Syria initially to disrupt using air power, and eventually to pressure using a moderate opposition, then I think we place ISIL in an untenable position. And in the middle of that, restore the border so they can't flow back and forth freely.

Senator REED. Thank you.

Thank you, Mr. Chairman.

Chairman LEVIN. Thank you, Senator Reed.

Senator McCain.

Senator McCAIN. Thank you, Mr. Chairman.

I thank the witnesses.

I understand that, according to your testimony, that we will be training and equipping approximately 5,000 in one year. Is that correct?

Secretary HAGEL. Yes.

Senator McCAIN. Is—and ISIL now—the estimates are that there are some 31,000 metastasizing in a very rapid fashion into a much larger force. To many of us, that seems like a inadequate response to what——

Chairman LEVIN. Would you please be quiet. I am asking you now to please leave the room. Please remove this lady. Please remove her. The disruptions are not going to be acceptable to anybody. They are not—they are not helping you in any way. Please remove the lady from the room. Thank you very much, to our officers. Thank you.

Senator McCAIN. I always appreciate special attention from this group, Mr. Chairman. [Laughter.]

Chairman LEVIN. Senator McCain.

Senator McCAIN. And obviously, this group of 5,000, as you mentioned, in unit-sized deployments will be back in Syria, fighting against ISIL. They will also be fighting against Bashar Assad, which they have been doing for a number of years before ISIL was ever a significant factor. Now, they will be fighting against Bashar Assad. And Bashar Assad will attack them from the air, which he has done, and with significant success, not only against them, but there's been 192,000 people who have been slaughtered in Syria since the onset. If a—if one of the Free Syrian Army is fighting against Bashar Assad, and he is attacking them from the air, would we take action to prevent them from being attacked by Bashar Assad?

Secretary HAGEL. Senator, let me begin. To the first part of your question, the 5,000.

Senator MCCAIN. I—dispense with that. I'd like to answer the question, Will we—if the Free Syrian Army units are attacked from the air by Bashar Assad, will we prevent those attacks from taking place and take out Bashar Assad's air assets, both helicopter and fixed wing, that will be attacking the Free Syrian Army units?

Secretary HAGEL. Well, we're, first of all, not there yet, but our focus is on ISIL. And that is the threat——

Senator MCCAIN. So we heard.

Secretary HAGEL.—right now to our country and to our interests and to the people of the region. So, what we are training these units for, yes, is a stabilizing force in Syria, as an option, but the first focus is, as I just said, as the President laid out in his statement to the country——

Senator MCCAIN. I take it from your answer that we are now recruiting these young men to go and fight in Syria against ISIL, but if they are attacked by Bashar Assad, we are not going to help them. Is that correct?

Secretary HAGEL. They will defend themselves, Senator.

Senator MCCAIN. Will we help them against Assad's air——

Secretary HAGEL. We will help them, and we will support them as we have——

Senator MCCAIN. How will we help them——

Secretary HAGEL.—trained them.

Senator MCCAIN. Will we repel Bashar Assad's air assets that will be attacking them?

Secretary HAGEL. Any attack on those that we have trained who are supporting us, we will help them.

Senator MCCAIN. I guess I am not going to get an answer. But, it seems to me that you have to neutralize Bashar Assad's air assets if you are going to protect these people that we are arming and training and sending in to fight.

Is that inaccurate, General Dempsey?

General DEMPSEY. The coalition we are forming, Senator, won't form unless—if we were to take Assad off the table, we would have a much more difficult time forming a coalition. But, I think what you are hearing us express is an ISIL-first strategy. I don't think we'll find ourselves in that situation, given what we intend to do with——

Senator MCCAIN. You don't think that the Free Syrian Army is going to fight against Bashar Assad, who has been decimating them? You think that these people you are training will only go back to fight against ISIL? Do you really believe that, General?

General DEMPSEY. What I believe, Senator, is that, as we train them and develop a military chain of command linked to a political structure, that we can establish objectives that defer that challenge into the future. We do not have to deal with it now.

Senator MCCAIN. That's a fundamental misunderstanding of the entire concept and motivation of the Free Syrian Army. The—it is Bashar Assad that has killed many more of them than ISIL——

General DEMPSEY. I agree.

Senator MCCAIN.—has. And for us to say that we are going to go in and help and train and equip these people, and only to fight against ISIL, you're not going to get many recruits to do that, General. I guarantee you that. And that's a fundamental fallacy in everything you are presenting the—this committee today.

General—Secretary Hagel, was the President right, in 2012, when he overruled most of his national security team and refused to train and equip the moderate opposition in Syria at that time?

Secretary HAGEL. Senator, I was not there at the time, so I am limited——

Senator MCCAIN. Well, I'll ask General Dempsey, then. He was there at the time.

General DEMPSEY. I am sorry, Senator, when you asked the question——

Senator MCCAIN. Was the President right, in 2012, when he overruled his Secretary of Defense, Secretary of State, and Director of the CIA, and refused to train and equip the moderate opposition forces in Syria, which, according to your testimony, we are doing today?

General DEMPSEY. Senator, you know that I recommended that we train them; and you know that, for policy reasons, the decision was taken in another direction.

Senator MCCAIN. Thank you.

Are you concerned, Secretary Hagel, about our southern border? We received testimony from our homeland security people that our border is porous and the people who are now free to travel to the United States and also other radical elements might cross our southern border to attack the United States.?

Secretary HAGEL. I am always concerned about——

Senator MCCAIN. I mean, is that a serious——

Secretary HAGEL.—our borders.

Senator MCCAIN.—concern of yours?

Secretary HAGEL. I think we have to always look at these things as——

Senator MCCAIN. Do you think we have to——

Secretary HAGEL.—serious concerns——

Senator MCCAIN. In other words, do you think we have to improve our border security, especially on the southern border?

Secretary HAGEL. We can improve our border security.

Senator MCCAIN. Thank you.

My time is expired.

Chairman LEVIN. Thank you very much, Senator McCain.

Senator Nelson.

Senator NELSON. Senator McCain, you're aware that there were published reports of covert training. Covert training.

Senator MCCAIN. I am aware of it. And I am also aware of the scale of the training that was required. And I am also aware of the situation today. And I am also aware 192,000 people have been slaughtered, a lot of them with these so-called "barrel bombs," which are—and the use of chlorine gas—which has caused a humanitarian disaster of incredible proportions. Yes, I am aware of that.

Senator NELSON. General Dempsey, are you aware of the published reports of covert training?

General DEMPSEY. Senator, I—we don't comment in public about any aspect of covert training.

Senator NELSON. Mr. Secretary, as you know, I believe that the President has the constitutional authority to go on and attack ISIS. This is going to be for the long haul. And eventually this issue will have to come to Congress for authorization for the use of military force. And you all have an appropriations request right now.

My question is, If Congress does not approve—and I have heard some Members of Congress say that they are not going to vote to approve this $500 million request—if they did that and refused before we adjourn to go home for the election, what kind of message do you think that sends?

Secretary HAGEL. Well, I think that message would be very, very seriously misunderstood and misinterpreted by our allies, our friends, our partners around the world, and our adversaries. This is a clear, clear threat, what the President has talked about, the threat to this country from ISIL, and what his request is, and reaching out to the Congress for partnership as he has done, in consultation with many, many Members of the Congress, to be partners in this effort to protect this country. And if the Congress would not agree to that request, it would be a pretty devastating message that we send to the world.

Senator NELSON. I happen to——

Chairman LEVIN. All right, all right, would you please—would you please not take advantage of the freedom of this place? And will you please remove this lady from the room? Thank you. This disruption is not helping either the facts to be known or helping your cause in any way.

Senator NELSON. As you know, Mr. Secretary, I've taken this position that I think he has the—he, the President—has the constitutional authority to go on and attack inside Syria. The fact that you're making this request, and, as you've testified here today, that you'll train up 5,000 over the course of the next year, does that basically mean any kind of coordinated effort on the ground in Syria is delayed for a year?

Secretary HAGEL. If we don't have ground capability in a moderate opposition, yes, it affects a rather significant dimension of the overall strategy.

Senator NELSON. As you know, some people are saying that attacking ISIS, both in Iraq and Syria, is playing into their hand by then them using that to divide Muslims against us. What is your opinion?

Secretary HAGEL. This is why the coalition, including, out front, publicly, Muslim Arab countries, is so critical to this. And I noted that in—I think in one or two of my answers this morning, as well as in my testimony.

Senator NELSON. Can you shed any more light—as ISIS, as one of the two of you have testified, recedes into an urban area and takes shelter there among a civilian population, how, in Iraq, for example, can the Iraqi Security Forces be able to root them out of that civilian territory?

Secretary HAGEL. Well, this, again, is why we need the people—why we need the people, themselves, in Iraq, in Syria, to support a unified unity, inclusive, representative government in Iraq to help them do that. The Sunni tribes are critical to this. What's allowed so much of this to happen, Senator, as you know, as you visited there many times, is—the last government in Iraq, over the last 5 years, have actually exacerbated the effort and intentionally destroyed the capability of a unity government to bring in the Sunni/Shi'a/Kurdish populations to a government that they would trust, that they could have confidence in, that they knew would work in everyone's interest. So, your question cuts directly to the overall effort, here, of what the President talked about in a new, inclusive unity government, which we have some confidence in, but we believe that a body will do. And, so far, in his appointments to his cabinet, we have seen evidence of that inclusiveness.

Chairman LEVIN. Thank you very much, Senator Nelson.

Senator Wicker.

Senator WICKER. Thank you.

Gentlemen, thank you for your testimony today.

Here's how I view it. The surge in Iraq, ordered by President George W. Bush, worked. President Obama rejected the advice of many of his top military leaders to leave a residual force. Our administration did not make every effort that it possibly could to gain a Status of Forces Agreement in Iraq. And so, we completely withdrew. And now ISIS is there, controlling large parts of the territory and wreaking the havoc that the President's responding to.

I am willing to help the President, and to help you gentlemen, take this hill again if I believe there is a plan that will work and be successful. If training 5,000 troops in—at the—by the end of one year is going to help us be successful against something that's already metastasized, and at 31,000, which is the size of ISIS now, I want to help, if we can be convinced it will work, and also if we can have some assurance that we will not throw away our gains this time, as we did after the surge worked.

General Dempsey, in answer to the question by the Chairman of this committee, "Do you support the President's strategy?" you say that you do. Now, the Washington Post reports that Mr. Obama has rejected the recommendation of his top military commanders that U.S. Special Operation Forces be deployed to assist Iraqi army units in fighting the rebels. Is that report by Rajiv Chandrasekaran correct, in the Washington Post? And where did you come down on that recommendation?

General DEMPSEY. No, that report is not correct. And where I came down on the recommendation, in terms of having advisors accompany—this is the issue we're describing, whether advisors, who are already there and generally resident in headquarters—whether they would accompany the Iraqi Security Forces into combat. I have not come to an occasion where I believe that's necessary. They are doing fine. We're able to provide them air power using full motion video and systems——

Senator WICKER. Who is doing fine?

General DEMPSEY. The Iraqi Security Forces and the Peshmerga are moving back on the offensive.

But, as I said, Senator, if I get to the point where, for a particular mission, I think they should accompany, I'll make that recommendation.

Senator WICKER. Yes, and I did hear you say that, and I at least appreciate that.

Let me submit for the record a column in today's Post, Mr. Chairman, by Marc Thiessen in—wherein he talks about General Lloyd Austin, a top commander, U.S. Forces in the Middle East. And to quote Mr. Thiessen, "In 2010, General Austin advised President Obama against withdrawing all U.S. forces from Iraq, recommending that the President instead leave 24,000 U.S. troops to secure the military gains made in the surge and to prevent a terrorist resurgence. Had Obama listened to Austin's counsel, the rise of the Islamic State could have been stopped." Where did you come down on that debate, General Dempsey, at that point?

General DEMPSEY. Well, actually, Senator, as you know, we don't debate anything in the military. We provide options and——

Senator WICKER. A discussion.

General DEMPSEY.—and let our elected officials make their decisions.

It's well known that all military leaders believed we needed to leave some residual force in Iraq to continue the development of the security forces. I—you know, there's a—there is a debate, in which I am not a participant, about whether we tried as hard as we could to leave it there. And that's a debate that will continue, I believe. But, I thought we should have left forces there. I traveled to Iraq, and I—I was the Chief of Staff of the Army at the time—discussed it with the Prime Minister.

Look, I don't know what—how history will exactly describe this. Let me describe Nouri al-Maliki as a very difficult partner most of the time, and in particular on that issue.

Senator WICKER. Well, on the issue of trying hard enough, I think anybody that's really observed the situation would acknowledge that a government—a U.S. Government that can go into Iraq today and persuade the Prime Minister to step down could certainly have mustered the skills to get them to sign a Status of Forces Agreement. So, it's obvious to me that we didn't try very hard.

And let me just reiterate to you, I want us to win. I want us to defeat ISIS. But, I want a plan that can be successful, and I am not sure 5,000 trained in a year can be successful against 31,000. And I want to make sure that we don't make the same mistake again by throwing those gains away.

One quick question to you, Secretary Hagel. In reading your testimony about what the coalition partners are going to do, I have no idea specifically what we are asking of them or what they're—what we can expect. They've expressed their willingness, they've indicated their readiness, they want to help, to do their share, begin making commitments, take measures to suppress the flow. I have no idea, based on your testimony, what our coalition partners are expected to do, or even what we want them to do.

Secretary HAGEL. Senator, my intent was not to give you that inventory this morning and go through that. First of all——

Senator WICKER. Are you able to?

Secretary HAGEL. We can do that privately, in closed session, with a number of countries. That's what we're doing right now. We're in the process of doing that right now. As I mentioned, over the last 2 weeks, we've been building the coalition. We've been organizing the coalition. General Allen's main job, as I noted in my testimony, is doing that right now. He's meeting with the President this morning. We have all finalized that effort. We have a list of over 40 nations who we have talked to. Most have come to us, who have volunteered specific areas of expertise, what they would do. We'll make specific requests. But, that's ongoing right now. That's part of the plan the President discussed——

Senator WICKER. Will Saudi pilots in Saudi jets be involved in airstrikes?

Secretary HAGEL. Like I said, it's part of the plan, and I don't want to get into the specifics of that in an open hearing. But, as I said in my testimony, as Secretary Kerry has said as recently as yesterday, we have Middle Eastern allies who have said that they will be involved in military operations with us. And, for right now, at an opening hearing, let me leave it——

Chairman LEVIN. Thank you——

Secretary HAGEL.—that way. But, let me assure you that that is going on right now, and it's a key part of what we need to do.

General DEMPSEY. And if I could assure the Senator that, when Lloyd Austin and I convene a Chief of Defense Conference soon, after the President approves the campaign plan—there's a couple of things we have to accomplish. One is, we need to make the campaign plan the Iraqi campaign plan, not CENTCOM's campaign plan. Second, the contributions of, in particular, the Arab nations need to be real. It can't—in our—and this is military, now. I'm not looking for political support, I'm looking for special forces advisors, I'm looking for trainers, I'm looking for tankers, I'm looking for ISR, and I'm looking for strike aircraft.

Chairman LEVIN. Thank you very much——

Senator WICKER. Thank you.

Chairman LEVIN.—Senator Wicker.

Senator McCaskill.

Senator McCASKILL. Just to clarify a different set of circumstances, when Maliki and the Government of Iraq told us to get out and refused to do a Status of Forces Agreement, I am pretty sure Iran was with them on that, correct? Iran was very close to Maliki, and Iran wanted us out of Iraq as much as the Iraqi government did at that point in time. Is that a correct assessment, Secretary Hagel and General Dempsey?

General DEMPSEY. Yes, I guess I'm stuck with this one because I was the one here, right? But—and here I am, I said I did not want to get into the debate; now I am in the debate.

You know what? I—who knows what was going through Prime Minister Maliki's head at the time. I mean, there was this—I mean, I can tell you from personal contact with him, he had a almost obsessive notion of his sovereignty——

Senator McCASKILL. Right.

General DEMPSEY.—and wanting to establish it. Was he influenced by Iran? Undoubtedly.

Senator McCASKILL. Right.

General DEMPSEY. But, it is pretty hard to say, Senator. But, what I——

Senator McCASKILL. But——

General DEMPSEY.—will tell you, he was a very reluctant partner.

Senator MCCASKILL. I guess the point I am trying to make is, it's a much different situation now, in terms of getting Maliki to step down. Iran was very concerned about ISIL taking over Iraq and what that meant. And clearly there was pressure being exerted for Maliki to step down, by Iran. So, us getting—I think, for us to take credit for getting Maliki to step down is unrealistic, in light of what the geopolitical forces were in their neck of the woods at that point in time.

Secretary HAGEL. I was here, on this episode, and I can tell that it wasn't the United States that pushed Maliki out; it was his own people, Iran being part of that. So, it wasn't the United States dictating that Maliki stay or not stay. Let's not forget that Iraq is a sovereign nation, it has elections. We may not like the outcomes, but it is a sovereign country. That was the entire point when General—or when President Bush signed the December 2008 agreement to leave Iraq.

Senator MCCASKILL. Right.

Secretary HAGEL. It was a sovereign nation. So, the United States didn't force or push, through some new system of influence, Maliki out. It was the people that made that decision.

Senator MCCASKILL. I want to touch on the issue of the Shi'a militia. As we looked at the surge, one of our successes in the surge was certainly our ability to bring over moderate Sunnis. And that was noted at the time and talked about a great deal, about our ability to finally get the cooperation of a lot of moderate Sunnis. Clearly, the moderate Sunnis have thrown in with ISIL because of the problems—political problems that they were confronted with, in terms of exclusion from the Iraqi government. So, the clerics put out the call to repel ISIL to the Shi'a militias, and they have been partially responsible for the successes that there have—that have occurred on the ground.

What are we doing? This is just one of many complex problems that presents itself in this tangle that we are in. And one of the most complex is, How are we going to deal with the empowerment of the Shi'a militia within the Iraqi Security Forces, moving forward, as we try to ultimately get a political solution, which is a unified government and security forces that represent all parts of that country?

General DEMPSEY. Couple of things, Senator. One is, you know, I'm a little reluctant—in fact, I try not to ever talk about "the Sunni" as a monolithic block. I mean, if the Senator's chart was still up there, it looks like ISIL has geographic objectives. It actually has tribal objectives. It eats its way tribe by tribe, wherever it goes. And the fact that it ends up in Mosul is actually more happenstance of the tribe they are trying to pursue. If we showed the tribes on that slide, there would probably be 48 to 54 different tribes that ISIL is—has, in some ways, coerced or coopted or driven away. So, the Sunni are not monolithic in any sense, and we have to remember that.

The second thing is, on your question about the Shi'a militia. Look, I think our offer of support, here, should—needs to—is—will be conditional. And that is, for example, there were 50 Iraqi brigades that we assessed. Twenty-six of them we assessed to be reputable partners. That is to say, they have remained multiconfessional, they are well led, they still have their equipment, they seem to have a certain cohesion and a commitment to the central government. The other 24 concerned us a bit on the issue of infiltration and leadership and sectarianism.

So, we can apply our support conditionally, and that's the way we influence the outcome I think you're discussing.

Senator MCCASKILL. Finally, if—I'm assuming that this is a contingency operation and wanted to point out that the new provisions of the war contracting legislation that have been put into law should be applicable for this effort. I know that there is some talk that you've asked for cost estimates for security assistance mentors and advisors in Iraq through a contracting platform. And I don't know, are we building training facilities in Saudi, the American government? And, if so, I just wanted to sound the alarm now, before rather than after, because usually I am hollering about after—I want to sound the alarm before, that all these contracting provisions that we've worked so hard to get into place, that we don't go down the road of mistakes that we have traveled so frequently around this contracting space in contingencies.

Secretary HAGEL. Well, I can assure you, Senator, that any commitments we made, in contracting or anything else, we will follow the law clearly and consult with Congress.

Senator MCCASKILL. Thank you.

Chairman LEVIN. Thank you, Senator McCaskill.

Senator Ayotte.

Senator AYOTTE. Thank you, Mr. Chairman.

I want to thank both of you for your service during these challenging times.

I wanted to follow up, General Dempsey, on a question that Senator Wicker had asked you about, about providing our advisors or our Special Forces, embedding them with the Iraqi forces. And I believe you said that you don't believe that that is necessary right now. Would you agree with me, though, that airstrikes are much more effective with having our Special Forces, or having a sort of JTAC capability, in terms of the effectiveness of strikes on the ground, with our people?

General DEMPSEY. It depends on the kind of contact that the two forces are having. And let me explain.

When the two forces are separate, when ISIL is at some geographic separation from the Iraqi Security Forces, it's not very difficult at all to discriminate between the targets.

Senator AYOTTE. Sure. But, when—isn't our problem with when they are not out in open space, when we have to distinguish between, for example, civilian targets and——

General DEMPSEY. That is correct.

Senator AYOTTE.—military targets, that——

General DEMPSEY. Yes.

Senator AYOTTE.—our people are very effective at that?

General DEMPSEY. Yes, absolutely. And that is where I was headed. If they—if we get into a circumstance where the forces are very intermingled, then the target discrimination becomes more difficult.

But, I will say, this isn't a light switch, either you do it or you don't. There are technologies available, that we didn't have 5 years ago, that allow us to actually apply force and to see the situation on the ground in ways we couldn't before. But, I'm—I'm not walking away from what I said. If we get to the point where I think we need the JTAC with the Iraqi Security Forces, I'll make the recommendation. But, I'm not there.

Senator AYOTTE. You do not think we need that at this time?

General DEMPSEY. I do not.

Senator AYOTTE. Can I ask you a question? Does General Austin—has he made a recommend—what was his thought on this, given that he's the CENTCOM Commander and his prior experience in Iraq?

General DEMPSEY. We—on the Mosul Dam operation, the one I described earlier, which was very complicated, as much by the introduction of three—of the two different forces speaking two different languages, he did suggest that we should use the JTACs in an accompany role. As we discussed it and worked through it, he found a way to do it, as I described it to you.

Senator AYOTTE. So, he has not made recommend—so, he has not made recommendations, beyond the Mosul Dam operation, that we should embed our Special Forces or, certainly, JTAC capability——

General DEMPSEY. Not at this time.

Senator AYOTTE.—with the forces?

General DEMPSEY. No, he shares my view that there will be circumstances when we think that'll be necessary, but we haven't encountered one yet.

Senator AYOTTE. Well, I think we've had experience this—with this, though, haven't we, prior in Iraq, with having our forces embedded, and also with Afghanistan, of our people being quite effective, in terms of targeting the airstrikes? You would agree with me?

General DEMPSEY. Absolutely. We know how to do that.

Senator AYOTTE. Yes. I think that I certainly—thinking about as we are dealing with civilian populations, I'm not confident how this is going to happen without the assistance of our trained special operators on the ground, here.

But, I appreciate that you've said that you have not ruled this out.

General DEMPSEY. I have not, in terms of recommendations.

Senator AYOTTE. Thank you. Has the President ruled it out?

General DEMPSEY. Well, at this point, he's—his stated policy is that we will not have U.S. ground forces in direct combat. So, yes.

Senator AYOTTE. Including operators and JTAC and—embedded on the ground.

General DEMPSEY. That's correct. But, he has told me, as well, to come back to him on a case-by-case basis.

Senator AYOTTE. So, let me ask you about the threat that we face, Secretary Hagel, General Dempsey. So, General Allen, who I have great respect for, and I know both of you do, as well, he has been appointed the Special Presidential Envoy for the global coalition to counter ISIL. And we all know his experience, not only in Iraq, but in Afghanistan. So, he has described, in August, ISIS as—or, ISIL as a clear and present danger to the United States. Do you agree with his characterization?

Secretary HAGEL. Senator, I was asked the question earlier, whether I agreed, still, with what I had said. I—my words were quoted back to me about an imminent threat to America's interests around the world. And I said, yes, I do, ISIL is a threat to America, our allies, our interests around the world. I'm not going to answer for General Allen, but I think we all agree, at least within the administration—General Allen, General Dempsey, General Austin, me, the President, others—that ISIL is a threat. I said that in my testimony. The President of the United States said it last week in his speech.

Senator AYOTTE. Well, do you believe it's a present threat to us?

Secretary HAGEL. Well, a present threat, meaning they murdered two Americans over the last couple of weeks. I'd say that's a pretty imminent threat.

Senator AYOTTE. Yes, I would agree——

Secretary HAGEL. And other threats that they have in—and how they threaten us——

Senator AYOTTE. Well, as you know, our prayers continue to go out to the Foley and Sotloff families, who—Jim Foley was from New Hampshire, and Steven Sotloff went to school in New Hampshire, so I believe it's an absolute clear and present threat to us.

Let me ask you about the Americans who have joined. In Homeland Security Committee last week, we had testimony from our top homeland security officials, as well as from the FBI, about the 100 Americans that have either gone to Syria or attempted to go to Syria. And what I learned was that this is not a firm number. How confident are we that we have track of these individuals, that we know that there's only 100 involved?

And I would ask the same question with regard to those who are holding Western passports, where we know that many of those countries—unfortunately, Jim Foley's murderer, as you know, had a British accent, and we have a—we're—have a visa waiver program with Great Britain. So, how confident are—we are in those numbers, as we look at this homeland threat, the ability and track of those individuals to come back to the United States of America in some way.

Secretary HAGEL. Well, Senator, I think, like any of these threats, they're—they always present imperfect situations. And when you ask "how confident," well, we are as confident as we can be, but you're constantly working at trying to make it better, more secure. I announced in—today in my testimony, it was announced a couple of days ago, what we're doing with Homeland Security, what we're doing with Justice, what we're doing with our Border Patrol, in coordination with all of these other nations, on identifying these individuals that we do know, or we are pretty sure of, are in the Middle East, Syria or wherever. There may be some we don't know. But, we're constantly refining and focusing on this. I don't think we can ever be too confident that we've got it all. But, we have some confidence that we do have the numbers about right.

Senator AYOTTE. Well, I thank you. My time is up. But, what I heard in the Homeland Security Committee last week did not give me a great degree of confidence, in terms of what we don't know, because the FBI has basically said that 100 number could be many more; and also we know less, even, about those where we do not always have full intelligence-sharing with all the Western passport-holders. So——

Secretary HAGEL. No, that's right.

Senator AYOTTE.—I think this is a real issue for us.

Secretary HAGEL. It is an issue.

Senator AYOTTE. Thank you.

Secretary HAGEL. Thank you.

Chairman LEVIN. Thank you.

Senator Wicker made a request, that I failed to acknowledge, that a column from the Washington Post be inserted in the record. It will be inserted in the record.

I will also insert in the record Secretary Gates's paragraph, which reads as follows in his book, "In the end, the Iraqi leadership did not try to get an agreement through their parliament that would have made possible a continued U.S. military presence after December 31. Maliki was just too fearful of the political consequences. Most Iraqis wanted us gone," close quote.

[The information referred to follows:]

[COMMITTEE INSERT]

Chairman LEVIN. Senator Udall.

Senator UDALL. Thank you, Mr. Chairman.

Good morning, gentlemen.

It is very clear that ISIL presents a very serious threat to U.S. interests and allies in the Middle East, and the group's actions have left no doubt that it's going to take both brains and brawn to defeat them. We've got to hit them hard. We've got to deny them safe haven. And we have to bring strategic capabilities of the United States and a committed international alliance to bear against them. And we need to work with our partners on the ground to eliminate the conditions that have allowed this cancer to spread so quickly. And the rise of ISIL should serve as a warning to leaders throughout the Middle East. And I would urge, as I think we all have, that the new Iraqi government must take immediate steps to move past the shortsighted and harmful policies that have contributed to the current crisis.

This is going to take our best effort. I know we have it in us. And we do need to get it right.

So, General Dempsey, in that spirit, let me direct a question to you. In order to defeat this enemy, we will need to be tough and smart. And you noted, last month, that defeating ISIL will require all application of all tools of national power: diplomatic, economic, information, and military. Could you describe how these tools would be used as part of a well-planned international effort to confront this threat?

General DEMPSEY. First, let me align myself with your assertion that an inclusive Government of Iraq that reconciles with the three—that reconciles the three major groups—Sunni, Shi'a, and Kurd—is absolutely a necessary precondition to the defeat of ISIL inside of Iraq.

And so, to your point, there has to be a—an integration of diplomatic, economic, in the sense of support for the Government of Iraq, as well as counterfinancing efforts so that the money that a Senator previously described that ISIL is garnering every day can be interdicted, tracked, and disrupted, the flow of foreign fighters.

And those are kind of strategic regional issues, really, because ISIL knows no boundaries, you know, knows no borders. So, we have—we absolute—it's not a matter of convenience that we form a coalition, it's a matter of necessity.

And then tactically—that is strategically—tactically, we have got to get enough of the Iraqi Security Forces and enough of the Peshmerga to go from defense to offense, to put it about as bluntly as we can. And, as we do, the Government of Iraq has to fill in behind that.

So, I mean, to be candid, there's some risk, here, that the—the three big risks that I would mention to you are if the Government of Iraq fails to become inclusive—and, though the signs are promising, they haven't yet fully delivered; second, if a coalition forms, but doesn't have endurance—because this is going to take several years; and then the third risk is retribution—you know, when the—when we encourage and assist the Iraqi Security Forces and the Pesh to regain lost territory, we have to be alert for the fact that, unless the Government of Iraq is there to embrace the people and show that they work together, there could be some retribution on the part of those who may have been seen as complicit with ISIL.

So, we've got some challenges ahead, but we are open-eyed to them, and I think we've got a good campaign plan.

Senator UDALL. I'd follow up on that. You've got significant experience on the ground in Iraq, and I think you know the region as well as anyone. Our military will be able to provide advice and assistance, clearly, but can you explain the reasons why it's important for the Iraqi Security Forces to take the lead in fighting back against ISIL on the ground?

General DEMPSEY. The author, Tom Friedman, has a famous saying, that no one in the history of mankind has ever washed their rental car. And I find that to be a good way to remember that ownership is ultimately what measures commitment. And I think it's clear that they have to own this—with our help and with the help of regional partners, but they have to own it.

Senator UDALL. I talked with Senator Graham last week, and we were discussing the fact that it's, I think, now time for the Arab leaders to really, truly step up. If this isn't an existential threat to them, it's certainly close to one. And I think that's what you are saying and what we're saying, as the United States.

Mr. Secretary, good to see you. Do you consider ISIL to be an associated force of al Qaeda? And could you explain your reasoning?

Secretary HAGEL. It has been an associated force of al-Qaeda. It has, over time, essentially displaced al Qaeda. But, there are still affiliations, to this day. But, it has been associated with al Qaeda.

Senator UDALL. General Dempsey, let me turn back to you. We've been talking about Syria. It's, I think, one of the most complex military environments we've ever seen. And, as you plan the mission to train and equip moderate Syrian opposition forces, how does the DOD define "moderate," and how do we take further steps to ensure that the weapons and the training we provide won't fall into the hands of these extremists groups?

General DEMPSEY. Well, Senator, I'd suggest to you that, though I recommended doing this a couple of years ago, we've—we learned a lot in the intervening time. We've learned a lot because of the nonlethal assistance we've provided, because we've had to make contacts with certain groups in order to flow that nonlethal assistance. And we've learned a lot, as well, from our coalition partners who have been interacting with the Free Syrian Army. We also have learned some lessons in vetting in places like Iraq and Afghanistan. We are very closely partnered with our intelligence agencies. And so, I would suggest to you that we've come a long way in our ability to vet.

In terms of defining a moderate opposition, I don't think that'll be as—I don't think that'll be difficult, actually. The region has become so polarized that those who are radical in their ideologies have made their move, and those that have not have actually demonstrated great courage in not making a move.

So, I think we'll be able to find the moderate opposition. I hope we can find them in the right numbers.

By the way, the 5,400 is capacity. It's just what we can throughput at several training bases in the course of a year. As the Secretary said, it's not the desired end state for a moderate Syrian opposition.

One last thing about developing a Syrian opposition. It really needs to be developed with a chain of command responsive to some Syrian political structure, not responsive to us. These can't be simply surrogates and proxies; they have to be tied, linked to some political structure that ultimately could assist in the governing of Syria when, finally, the Assad regime is either overthrown or, through the negotiation, is changed.

So, the important difference in what we're trying to do, here, is build a force that can, over time, actually contribute to stability in Syria, not just fight.

Senator UDALL. Thank you, gentlemen.

Chairman LEVIN. Thank you, Senator Udall.

Senator Vitter.

Senator VITTER. Thank you, Mr. Chairman.

Thank you both for your service, very much.

Did either or both of you give the President any advice regarding a possible new AUMF? And, if so, what was it?

Secretary HAGEL. Senator, obviously the question of authority was asked early on as we developed a strategy and our advice to the President. Does he have the constitutional authority which he believes he does? And his legal counsel told him he did. Does he have the statutory authority, which he believes he does, and he has said that as to his legal counsel saying the same thing. And we believe that—the same, that he has both statutory and constitutional authority. So, that was a recommendation that I made.

He also noted, as you recall from last week's statement to the American public, that he welcomed any additional authority that the President would give him, because he, feeling strongly that it is important that a strong partnership between Congress and the President always be established and always be seen in the eyes of the world.

Senator VITTER. Let me restate my question. You're saying he has legal authority without a new AUMF. A new AUMF could, nevertheless, be helpful. Did either or both of you give him advice about whether to seek one?

Secretary HAGEL. Well, I'll speak for myself, and the Chairman can answer it. I did not advise him to seek any additional authority. I asked our general counsel and our attorneys what they thought, but I did not specifically say to——

Senator VITTER. General?

General DEMPSEY. No, I haven't had a conversation in the interagency about whether—what a new AUMF would look like.

Senator VITTER. Okay. The current estimate of ISIS fighters is about 35,000. Is that correct?

General DEMPSEY. I think the last number I saw was actually 31-, but it's an inexact science because of the fact that these—as I said, the—there are tribes that are coopted.

Senator VITTER. Right.

General DEMPSEY. Sometimes they would be counted in that number, but their heart's not in it.

Senator VITTER. And that number——

General DEMPSEY. But, the latest number is 31,000.

Senator VITTER.—in the low- to mid-30s——

General DEMPSEY. Right.

Senator VITTER.—is clearly a huge growth over the last several months, correct?

General DEMPSEY. It is. And I assess it's growth because of their success. So, the reporting probably lags facts on the ground. And when that report was assembled, they were at their height of success.

Senator VITTER. And what's your best guesstimate about what it might be a year from now?

General DEMPSEY. I haven't formed one, so I'd be happy to take that one for the record.

[The information referred to follows:]

[INFORMATION]

Senator VITTER. Okay. And, given that number, and presumably increasing numbers, I take it everyone agrees some fighting force on the ground on the other side is necessary. What do you think that number has to be over time?

General DEMPSEY. Do you mean the other side of the border, sir, or do you mean——

Senator VITTER. No, no, no. I mean our side of the fight——

General DEMPSEY. Oh.

Senator VITTER.—against ISIS.

General DEMPSEY. I think that the—in Iraq, I think the combined forces of that part of the Iraqi Security Forces we assess to be—remain viable, and the Pesh, is adequate to the task of defeating ISIL in Iraq. I have concerns about the Syria side of this, for obvious reasons.

Senator VITTER. And again, what do you think the Syrian number on our side of the fight needs to move to?

General DEMPSEY. The problem on the Syrian side is less about how big the moderate opposition should become and more about how the—the lack of a inclusive government in Damascus affects the equation. In other words, the environment inside of Syria remains ripe for groups like ISIS because of the unwillingness of the

Syrian regime to reach out to the Sunni population, which makes it challenging to determine how big a ground force would have to be.

Senator VITTER. I mean, do you have any number in mind, any guesstimate about, as we speak, what would be a minimal optimal ground force?

General DEMPSEY. Some time ago when this came up, in looking at the kind of tasks that we might assign to a force of that size, to include, for example, restoring the Syrian side of the Iraq/Syria border, the number that our military planners were considering was about 12,000.

Senator VITTER. Okay. Besides training up Syrians on our side, what are the plans to add to that number to come up with a significant fighting force on our side in Syria?

General DEMPSEY. Besides the training and equip mission we've just described——

Senator VITTER. Right.

General DEMPSEY.—or we're describing?

Senator VITTER. I mean, I take it the training and equip mission we're all in favor of can't approach that number anytime soon, that we know of.

General DEMPSEY. That's why I've said, consistently, this takes a persistent and enduring commitment. But, not anytime soon, that's correct.

But, I'll tell you, if you're asking me, "How does the opposition in Syria finally prevail on—against ISIL?"—I think it's going to require the assistance of, in particular, Jordanians and probably some of the Syrian Kurds and probably the Turks.

Senator VITTER. And, going back to the overall ISIS number of 31- or 35,000, what percentage of that would you guesstimate is in Syria?

General DEMPSEY. About two-thirds.

Senator VITTER. So, great majority in Syria.

Okay, thank you, Mr. Chairman.

Chairman LEVIN. Thank you, Senator Vitter.

Senator Hagan.

Senator HAGAN. Thank you, Mr. Chairman.

And, Secretary Hagel and General Dempsey, thank you for your service.

I am pleased that the strategy that the administration has developed for defeating ISIS does include the training and equipping the moderate Syrian opposition. This is something that I've pushed for over a year, in part to prevent the power vacuum among the rebels that would allow a group like ISIS to gain strength. Air power alone, while important, does not win a conflict like this.

Reports of nearly 40 nations agreeing to support the fight against ISIS are a promising signal. And, while ISIS presents a severe threat to our National security, it's—also threatens many countries around the world, especially those in the Middle East. The U.S. cannot bear this fight alone, and a strong coalition, including the neighboring Arab states, is obviously critical to destroying ISIS.

Secretary Hagel, what is the administration's plan for going after the funding streams that are supporting ISIS? For example, it's been reported recently that anywhere between $1 to $2 million a day is revenue that's coming in to ISIS from oilfields and refineries that they have taken over and that they now control. Moving this oil doesn't happen in a vacuum. Can you share if and how the U.S. is going after this funding stream and then any other funds that are available to ISIS?

Secretary HAGEL. Senator, as you recall in my testimony this morning, I mentioned specifically what the Treasury Department is doing to coordinate this effort to go after the funding sources of ISIL. You mentioned oil, black-marketing oil through porous borders. That's one of the obvious areas of funding. As you, I'm sure, know, ISIL has gotten control of small oilfields, and that's obviously where it starts. But, they are multisourced through kidnapping and ransom and as they have gone into towns and cities over the last few months and decimated those areas, and raided banks and taken possession of great numbers of equities.

So, there is no one answer. It is a multinational effort that our Treasury Department is leading, along with our State Department. But, be assured that it is a premium focus to cut off resources for ISIL. And it's a premium focus for our strategy.

Senator HAGAN. You know, I think that's very important, because it certainly would degrade their capability.

I also think it's critical that the people of Syria have an alternative other than ISIS or other radical terrorist groups like it or the Assad regime. And that's why I have been pushing the administration to empower and arm the moderate Syrian opposition. While a strong moderate military force is essential, I do believe success on the battlefield can only set the condition for the political solution in Syria.

And, General Dempsey, you were just speaking about this, in particular, who will actually be the leader of this moderate Syrian opposition force. And so, my question is, Who is ultimately going to lead the force that the U.S. and our partner nations train and equip, both politically and military? And what is your current assessment of these capabilities? And then, what are the plans to develop the leaders that would form the backbone of a longer-term government?

General DEMPSEY. Thanks, Senator. The—one of the—we believe, one of the advantages of undertaking an overt—we call it "Title 10"—train-and-equip mission is, it's going to force that issue. It's going to force the Syrian Opposition Committee, the Syrian National Congress to find some way to establish a responsible political architecture into which this military force can plug in a way that the other effort has never actually forced. The other effort, largely deal with through intelligence channels, doesn't have the—kind of the forcing function that an overt program will have.

So, I think the first step is to conduct an overt program. Second, as part of the program, I can assure you that we will not only be training riflemen, but also training leaders so that there is a military chain of command to whom these Syrian fighters are responsive. So, they're not responsive to General Dempsey or Captain Dempsey, they're going to be responsive to Syrians. Because, again, the effort, here, is to allow them to take ownership for this in a way that, heretofore, I don't think they've had the opportunity to do so.

Senator HAGAN. Thank you.

News reports suggest that there could be many Westerners, even Americans, that might be fighting with ISIS. Needless to say, that's a serious concern, since it certainly has the potential to create more of a direct threat to the U.S. and our Western—European allies. Can you—do you see the presence of radicalized Westerners fighting with ISIS and the Khorasan as a threat to the U.S.? And, if so, is there a part of our strategy that seeks to disrupt their ability to recruit new members from the West?

General Dempsey.

General DEMPSEY. Of course I see it as a threat. The radicalization—the thing that sets ISIL apart is, in fact, its radical ideology. It's—you know, there's another question about whether they're an affiliate of al Qaeda. Well, they have been al Qaeda. They were al-Qaeda in Iraq. But, they became so radical that, actually, al Qaeda rejected them. I still consider them to be part of the al-Qaeda ideology, but with a much more apocalyptic, of you will, world view.

I don't think—you know, it's not all 31,000, clearly. But, enough of them that, were they to be able to achieve it—and unless some of the governments in the region can find a way to address the social issues inside of their countries, then the seductive nature of that vision becomes actually the most dangerous part of it, which is why their momentum has to be reversed.

Senator HAGAN. Thank you.

Chairman LEVIN. Thank you very much——

Senator HAGAN. Thank you.

Chairman LEVIN.—Senator Hagan.

Senator Fischer.

Senator FISCHER. Thank you, Mr. Chairman.

And thank you, gentlemen, for the challenges that you're facing and the options you're presenting to Congress on this.

General Dempsey, Congress is being asked to fund training for about 5,000 moderate Syrian rebels. If Congress would provide that funding immediately, how long do you think it would take before a program's going to be up and running? I realize there is a lot of variables involved in this. You need to find the folks that we're going to be training. You need to thoroughly vet them to make sure they are the fighters that we need and that we desire.

Also, how do the moderates leave the field of battle? How are they going to defend that territory in Syria while they're being trained? How are they going to defend that against Assad? If you could address that, please.

General DEMPSEY. To the first part of your question, Senator, we think 3 to 5 months to establish the program. Some of that is consumed by contracting for equipment. It's not as much, you know, maneuvering people into the right place. But, during that period of time, as well, we would have to, with the help of, in particular, some of our regional partners, recruit and vet. But, 3 to 5 months, and then deliver a capability sometime between 8 and 12 months. So, that's kind of the timeframe that we're working toward.

To your question about, "Will they come to be trained?"—in many cases, they've already been driven out of their homes and out of their villages by ISIL, or by the regime, in some cases, so we think we'll be recruiting mostly from displaced populations. And therefore, it won't be as though they're giving up the security of their families to come and train with us.

Senator FISCHER. Sir, I believe this is the first request from the administration, but it will not be the last. We're looking at 5,000 fighters now. We're looking at a growing force by ISIL that's, as you've estimated, is 31,000. Over this period of months where we're going to be training—finding people, vetting, training them, that will only grow, in my opinion.

As we look at this request, I believe it should be separate from the CR. I think it's very important that Congress have a full debate on it. I know you probably have nothing to say on how we do our business here, but I believe we need to be honest with the American people on what lies ahead. And, with the request as it is, we are not being honest with the American people.

If we truly are going to defeat ISIL, to degrade them and to defeat them, it's not just this one request. Do you anticipate that the President will be sending more requests to Congress? And, if so, when may we expect to see those?

Secretary HAGEL. I know you're anxious to answer.

Secretary HAGEL. Well, I always like to respond to a fellow Nebraskan.

The reason that I'm going to answer first is because this really puts the General in a more difficult position than he should be in. So, he may want to add something, but let me answer this way.

First, because I do know a little something about your institution, if it was a perfect world and if we didn't have the time constraints that we all are under, and you weren't all scheduled to go out, here, of session, here, in a couple of days, and the world was more perfect, I agree, this deserves—should have a thorough airing with the American people.

Senator FISCHER. If I can just interrupt you——

Secretary HAGEL. Yes.

Senator FISCHER.—on that. Just because we're scheduled—just because we're scheduled to go out on Thursday, we don't have to go out on Thursday, do we, sir?

Secretary HAGEL. Well, that's not a decision for me to make, nor a recommendation. That falls clearly on your side of the dais.

But, that said, if we would not get the authority now, we would lose a considerable amount of time. And I know it's imperfect. It was never meant to jam anyone or to put anybody in a tough spot. But, it is my opinion—I think the President's been pretty clear on this—that the time is of the essence, here. And, when the Congress comes back—and obviously when you come back, I assume there will have been an election and start forming a new Congress—there will be a debate, there should be a debate about this.

As to your questions, "What further requests might be coming?" Senator, right now the President has been as straightforward and honest with you, with the American people, as I have been. There's no hidden agenda, here, or we're waiting for another shoe to drop in a—on a request. No. I can't guarantee you, at all—I don't think you would want your Secretary of Defense to say, "I'm sorry, there—this is the end. No more." I think General Dempsey's point in some of his answers this—here this morning, he certainly will recommend if he thinks we need some more capabilities somewhere.

Senator FISCHER. Right.

Secretary HAGEL. That's what you want.

Senator FISCHER. Right.

Secretary HAGEL. And that's the way I would answer your question.

Senator FISCHER. I would say, as a fellow Nebraskan, that, when I traveled the State for 3 weeks in August, all across the State, for the first time I heard Nebraskans talk about foreign policy and ask questions about foreign policy. We didn't hear that in any campaign, any debates, any forums. But, people in Nebraska are focused on this, they know it's a concern. They are frightened, but they want this addressed in a way that we know the enemy is going to be defeated. And they expect us to do our job. If that means staying here longer, then we need to do that.

Thank you.

Thank you, Mr. Chairman.

Chairman LEVIN. Thank you, Senator Fischer.

Senator Manchin.

Senator MANCHIN. Thank you, Mr. Chairman.

And I want to thank both of you all for your continued service to the great country.

I agree with my Senator—my colleague, Senator Fischer—I agree wholeheartedly with her. We should stay here, and it should be separated. And it's a big enough issue for us to have a policy discussion and not be tied into the funding discussion that we're going to have with the CR. But, with that being said, it is what it is.

I have a hard time with all of this. And my problem is—and I think I've spoke to both of you—when I go home to West Virginia, the same as Nebraska, the same as anywhere else in the country, people say, "What do you expect to be different than what you've done in that region of the world for 13 years? If money or military might hasn't changed it, what makes you think you can change it now?" And when you start looking at what we've spent, almost $20 billion, trying to build up a 280,000-person army in Iraq, and the first time they were tested, they turned tail and ran, turned over the arsenal that we equipped them with, now is being used against us. Anyone seeing the video of ISIS taking all that back into Syria—it is absolutely appalling for us to look at that. And then when you look at we have done in that part of the world, a total of, in Iraq, $818 billion—this is—these are the figures I have—818 billion has been spent, 747 in Afghanistan, and growing; 1.6 trillion to date, and growing; 4,400 lives lost in Iraq, 36,000 wounded; 2200 lives in Afghanistan, and 21,000 wounded.

The only thing I'm saying is, is—I understand Syria. It's a sectarian war, conflict against the Assad regime. So, everybody in there, whoever they may be, is fighting Assad, the way I understand it. If they're all fighting Assad, even though they might not be united—they all know they're trying to get rid of the Assad regime—we're supposed to carve out 5,000, 3,000, 5,000. At $100,000 per person, if my math is correct—5 billion—or $500 million for 5,000, correct? Okay. So, that's 100,000 per person that we're supposed to do. Only thing that I know that we're assured of is, that training and those weapons will probably be used against us at some time in the future if everything that's happened in the past— I have a hard time understanding why all of a sudden we're going to convince these 5,000 to turn and fight ISIS, who's fighting the same religious war that they're fighting against the Assad regime. Doesn't make any sense.

I'm in total support of air support, of using our tactical and our technology, as we have, for superiority. But, I think it should be the Arab Muslim ground game, if you would. That should be theirs. If we can booster them up a little bit—and you said we had to go back in, then either we've done a poor job of training in the beginning or Maliki was able to undo everything we did in the first— the 2 years that he—that we've been gone. If it's that quickly undone, what we have spent, what makes anybody—how can you all explain to me—how can I go home to West Virginia and make sense out of this at all?

Anybody want to take a shot at this? I—you know, it just doesn't make sense to me.

Secretary HAGEL. Well, if you put it that way, Senator. [Laughter.]

Well, first, I understand, I think, a lot of the complications. And we are dealing with the same issue. So, I don't minimize at all what you're saying as you try to explain this to the people you represent. But, let me make a couple of points.

First, it's not the United States alone that's going to change all this. This is the whole point of what the President talked about in his statement to the American public last week. We are going to help empower the people of Iraq. We are going to do everything we can to support their efforts with a new government, inclusive government. You mentioned the squandering of the last 5 years of the Maliki government, which has brought a great deal of this on.

Senator MANCHIN. But, you said that that's—they're a sovereign nation, so we don't have—we don't like the outcome, but they have a process.

Secretary HAGEL. They have a process. This——

Senator MANCHIN. That can be changing. That can change continuously.

Secretary HAGEL. That's right. And we're hopeful that this new government is going to put them back on a road of responsible, responsive, representative government. We are not going to have ground forces on the ground to do it for them. As you said——

Senator MANCHIN. No, I——

Secretary HAGEL.—it should be the—it should be the people of that region, of the country. As the Chairman noted, the Peshmerga, Iraqi Security Forces have been able to get back on the offensive, with our assistance.

Senator MANCHIN. But, those forces are able—and I'm so sorry, Mr. Secretary, I know our—you know, how time runs here—those forces have been able, let's say, to maybe hold the ground a little bit in their own territories, but they're not going to be moving into Syria. ISIS——

Secretary HAGEL. Well, that's why——

Senator MANCHIN. ISIS——

Secretary HAGEL.—that's why we need—we need a ground game——

Senator MANCHIN. Yes.

Secretary HAGEL.—in Syria——

Senator MANCHIN. But, ISIS hasn't been——

Secretary HAGEL.—of the people there.

Senator MANCHIN.—ISIS hasn't been able to—I mean, they've tried to take out Assad, correct? Is it fair to say that ISIS has tried to take out Assad?

Secretary HAGEL. ISIS has tried to take out everybody and——

Senator MANCHIN. But, Assad. And they have——

Secretary HAGEL.—everyone around it, but——

Senator MANCHIN.—they failed——

Secretary HAGEL.—they're a threat to us. I think that's the main point that—Senator, that is important for you, but for all of us. ISIS is a—ISIL is a threat to the United States.

Senator MANCHIN. But, Assad is not a threat to the United States.

Secretary HAGEL. Well, it's not the same kind of threat. I mean, what he—what he's allowed to happen in his own country——

Senator MANCHIN. I agree, it's——

Secretary HAGEL.—is why we've got a——

Senator MANCHIN.—it's barbaric also.

Secretary HAGEL.—problem in Syria.

Senator MANCHIN. But, here's what I'm just saying. I'm concerned about the United States of America. I'm concerned about West Virginia and all 49 other States and everybody that lives in those States. I'm concerned about how we're keeping them, from here, to do harm to America or Americans are planning. I'm for all of that. Attack wherever may be. But, I'm just saying, our past performance for 13 years in that region hasn't given us the results. We took out Saddam. We thought that would change. Iraq's in worse shape. We've—take out Qaddafi. We thought that would change. It go so bad in Libya, we've had to pull out our own Embassy and our people in our Embassy. They're wanting to take out—these barbaric dictators are unbelievable, but it seems like that's what rules. If it's not one, it'll be another. We're taking out a person—are turning our efforts to ISIS, who were Assad. I'm not supporting, any way, shape, or form, Assad. Think he should be gone. But, as long as he's able to remain there, he's fighting the same people that we're asking the people to train to fight that we're going to spend $500 million. Makes no sense to me, and I can't sell it. I've tried on my—you can't sell this stuff. And no who believes the outcome will be any different.

General, do you have anything to add to that?

General DEMPSEY. Yes, could I, Mr. Chairman? This is important enough that——

Chairman LEVIN. Of course.

General DEMPSEY.—I think we probably need to bleed over a little bit.

You know, if you look back at some of the—I've been in the job now 3 years. And when you look back over the course of that time, I've been pretty clear that we've got a generational problem, which is to say a 20-year problem. So, if it was 3 years ago, okay, maybe it's a 17-year problem in the Middle East as these strongmen have been overthrown. And what appeared to be for a moment in time a bit of a fledgling democratic movement has been hijacked, and it's been hijacked by some extraordinarily dangerous people—dangerous not just to the region, but transregionally and globally, as well.

And one of the things you can count on the United States military to recommend is that every—you know, to belabor the metaphor of ground game and other sports analogies—look, I'm always going to come to you and tell you what we need to play an away game. I don't want to play a home game.

I will promise you this. Left unaddressed, the issues in the Middle East will affect probably our European allies far more than us initially. And I believe they're awakening to that reality, by the way. There will be a period of unrest in the Middle East that initially will probably just be an economic challenge, but could ultimately actually threaten us directly here in the homeland.

And so, we have to—this is actually—we don't have a choice. I mean, if I could wall up continental United States and somehow assure you that the people of West Virginia will remain safe, I would do it, Senator. But, we can't.

And so, we've got three tools in the military arsenal. One is, we can do things ourselves. We all that direct action. Second, we can build partners. Third, we can enable others, like we're doing with the French in Mali.

What we've tried to do over the past few years is do less ourselves, more with partners, and enable others. That's the right path. We should do less ourselves, enable partners, and build partners. But, if we fail to address all three, we're back to doing it all ourselves. And so, what we're suggesting here is a strategy, where we can get others, not only to do some of the lifting, but maybe pay for it, as well.

I think that's the message to the people of West Virginia. We have to do—we have to be engaged, because people—we are antithetical. Most of ISIL's ideology is antithetical to our values. And so, you just can't let them fester.

Question is, Do we do it ourselves or try to do it with others? We're trying to do it with others. I think it's the right path.

Chairman LEVIN. Thank you very much, Senator Manchin.

Senator Graham.

Senator GRAHAM. Well, I think that's a good way to begin. I couldn't agree with you more. The goal is to destroy ISIL and all they represent. Is that correct?

General DEMPSEY. It is.

Senator GRAHAM. Very briefly, describe what destroying ISIL would look like, General Dempsey.

General DEMPSEY. Yes, I'm probably going to be a little more articulate about that in Iraq, because we've got a partner and we've got a credible ground force to enable.

Defeating or destroying ISIL in Iraq will require the combined forces of ISF and Pesh to go offensive, to regain lost territory, while concurrently—and this is the important part—the Government of Iraq fills in behind with inclusive policies addressing—you're well familiar with the complaints of the Kurds and——

Senator GRAHAM. Can't we just maybe speed up the——

General DEMPSEY. And then we restore the border——

Senator GRAHAM. Okay.

General DEMPSEY.—and then they're defeated.

Senator GRAHAM. No, no, I'm with you. You take all the territory they hold, you take Mosul and Fallujah away from them, you put an Iraqi military on the ground that will be loyal to the Iraqi people, not just to the Shi'as, you have an inclusive government in Baghdad, where the Sunni tribes will feel like they—they're better off playing politics in Baghdad than siding with ISIL. That's destroying their ability to regenerate in Iraq. Syria, we'll talk about in a minute. But, I want to continue the theme about why all this matters.

Is there any doubt in your mind, each of you, that if ISIL had the capability to kill millions of Americans, they would do so?

General DEMPSEY. There's no doubt in my mind. They'll kill anybody who doesn't conform to their narrow ideological bent.

Secretary HAGEL. I agree.

Senator GRAHAM. So, really, it's mankind against ISIL, it's just not us against ISIL or Sunni Arab states against ISIL. If you're a Christian in the region, they will kill you very quickly. Is that correct?

General DEMPSEY. Unless you convert.

Senator GRAHAM. Okay. Now, I guess what I'm trying to persuade my colleagues, that these problems only get worse over time. But, are they limited to the Mideast? Are there radical Islamists that we should worry about in Africa?

General DEMPSEY. Absolutely.

Senator GRAHAM. Does the authorization to use military force allow this administration to go in to attack AQIP in Yemen without a new authorization?

General DEMPSEY. It does. Anything affiliated with AQ.

Senator GRAHAM. Okay. I'm going to write you a letter and name the organization that we could not attack without a new AUMF. I just want to see how far this goes. I'm a very robust Article 2 guy, but I think this is a pretty robust reading of the current AUMF. But, I'm not going to stand in your way. We need to get this right.

Now, areas of agreement. Training the Free Syrian Army, you recommend we do that, with all of the complications that go with it.

General DEMPSEY. And with a coalition, I do.

Senator GRAHAM. Okay. So, now let's get to Syria. To destroy ISIL if two-thirds of ISIL is in Syria, do you agree that somebody's got to go in on the ground and dig them out eventually?

General DEMPSEY. Somebody——

Senator GRAHAM. Okay.

General DEMPSEY.—yes, sir.

Senator GRAHAM. And it's better for us to be part of that somebody than just to be the only ones doing it.

General DEMPSEY. Absolutely.

Senator GRAHAM. Can you think of an Arab army that you could form in the next year that you would have confidence that could go in and destroy ISIL in Syria, hold the territory without substantial American support?

General DEMPSEY. There are partners in the region who have very capable special operating forces, and I think the campaign would envision that they would participate. That would certainly be our ask of them to participate in a ground campaign.

Senator GRAHAM. My question is, Can you envision a coalition of Arab states that have the capabilities to go into Syria, defeat ISIL, hold the territory without substantial U.S. military support?

General DEMPSEY. As long as, Senator, you'll elaborate on what you mean by "substantial U.S. military support."

Senator GRAHAM. Getting them to the battlefield. How do they get there? What does it take to maintain a large army in the field? Do they have the intelligence capability if we don't help them? Do they have sufficient air power to win the day without our support? Do they have the special forces capabilities to go and kill the leaders of ISIL without us being on the ground?

General DEMPSEY. Well, I was with you until "without us being on the ground." Because, as I mentioned in previous testimony, I——

Senator GRAHAM. Well, it's easy. If you think they can do it without us being on the ground, just say yes.

General DEMPSEY. Yes.

Senator GRAHAM. Okay. What if they lose?

General DEMPSEY. Any campaign is built on assumptions. I just made one. And if the assumption proves invalid, then you have to readjust your——

Senator GRAHAM. What's the consequences of a Arab army going into Syria virtually on their own and getting beat by ISIL, to us?

General DEMPSEY. Yes, I wouldn't suggest virtually on your own. I think they'll be enabling support that we would have——

Senator GRAHAM. By us?

General DEMPSEY. Yes, I do think, yes.

Senator GRAHAM. Okay. Well, we're having a semantic problem here. But, the bottom line is, What does it mean to the world if we take on ISIL and they defeat the people we send in to take them all? That's a bad day for us, do you agree?

General DEMPSEY. It's a bad day for the region. Yes, sir.

Senator GRAHAM. It's a bad day for the world, isn't it?

General DEMPSEY. It is.

Senator GRAHAM. Do you agree with me this is probably our last best chance to put these guys in a box and keep them there?

General DEMPSEY. I think it's our last best chance to convince regional governments that if they don't solve their internal problems, we can't do it for them, and they'd better get serious about it.

Senator GRAHAM. What if the following happens: The regional players say that, "I don't trust the United States, because you've been so unreliable. You have drawn red lines and done nothing. You withdrew from Iraq and left the place in shambles, that I really don't want to follow your leadership, because I don't think you're capable of winning the war, because you don't have the resolve"? What if they tell us, "We're not going to do anything other than maybe drop a few bombs"? Would you consider the recommendation to the President that allowing ISIL to maintain a safe haven in Syria and to grow in capability over time is a major threat to the United States? Could you envision yourself recommending to the

President, if nobody else will help us, that we go in on the ground and clean these guys out in Syria? If we had to.

General DEMPSEY. You—yes, I haven't confronted that question yet, Senator, but I'll react to it. I don't think that, even were—if we were to go in and—on the ground, armored divisions with flags at furl——

Senator GRAHAM. The full weight of the military.

General DEMPSEY. I don't think we would do anything more than push this problem further to the right. This has got to be—to your point, if we don't get the kind of coalition I'm describing, then we're into a very narrow CT framework, in my view.

Senator GRAHAM. Okay. If I may just follow this point. So, our National defense, in terms of stopping ISIL from killing thousands or millions of Americans if they get the capability really comes down to whether or not we can convince the Arab world to go in there and defeat these guys?

General DEMPSEY. It really comes down to building a coalition so that what the Arab Muslim world sees is them rejecting ISIS, not us——

Senator GRAHAM. They already——

General DEMPSEY.—defeating them.

Senator GRAHAM.—reject ISIL. Do you know any major Arab ally that embraces ISIL?

General DEMPSEY. I know major Arab allies who fund them.

Senator GRAHAM. Yes, but do they embrace—they fund them because the Free Syrian Army couldn't fight Assad. They were trying to beat Assad. I think they realize the folly of their ways.

Let's don't taint the Mideast unfairly. Is it fair to say that most Syrians have two things in common: they don't like ISIL and they don't like Assad? Most Syrians.

General DEMPSEY. I agree.

Senator GRAHAM. Is it fair to say that most Muslims reject what ISIL does in the name of their religion?

General DEMPSEY. Yes.

Senator GRAHAM. Is it fair to say that if we don't contain this threat and eventually destroy it, that it gets worse over time and, a year from now, if they're still flourishing in Syria and this coalition hasn't come about, America is endangered of—more in danger of a major attack than we are today?

General DEMPSEY. Yes.

Senator GRAHAM. Thank you.

Chairman LEVIN. Okay.

Senator Shaheen.

Senator SHAHEEN. Thank you, Mr. Chairman.

And thank you, Secretary Hagel and General Dempsey, both for being here this morning and for your service.

I would like to direct my question, first, in a different direction. I think the barbarism and the threat that ISIL poses really became real for people in this country, certainly for people in New Hampshire, with the brutal murders of James Foley and Steven Sotloff. And, as Senator Ayotte has said, Jim Foley is from New Hampshire, and Steven Sotloff went to school there, so we saw that very personally, in terms of what happened.

I know that it has been reported that there was an effort to rescue the hostages who were being held by ISIL that was not successful. And I certainly commend all of the courageous servicemembers who were part of that effort. But, there have been reports, in recent news stories, from the Foley family that really raise, I think, very troubling and serious questions about the support that our Government provided to the families and to the effort to free Jim Foley and Steven Sotloff and the other hostages who are currently being held who are American citizens. Is there more that our Government can and should be doing to support the families and to looking at how we can help free hostages when they're being held in this situation?

Secretary HAGEL. Well, first, like all Americans, our thoughts and prayers go out to the families.

As to your question, Senator, as you know, Department of Defense does not have the direct——

Senator SHAHEEN. Right. I understand——

Secretary HAGEL.—contact——

Senator SHAHEEN.—that.

Senator SHAHEEN.—responsibility on this. However, that said, thank you for your comments about the rescue mission in—because it's an open hearing, we don't want to say too much more about it, but it's been in the press.

To your point about, "Can we do better and do more and is there an effort to address some of the more human dimensions of this?"—I'm not going to prejudge any of our departments and agencies in how they handle it, but I think we all must be mindful of the humanity, here, involved if it was our children or any of us personally in this situation. And I know our law enforcement people, those who have responsibility for dealing with this, it's a tough responsibility. They follow the law. But, I think we could and should maybe revisit some of the—some of these practices.

Now, the—our National security policy directive, as you know, is very clear on ransom. That's been in place for many, many years through different administrations. I'm not suggesting we change that, by the way.

Senator SHAHEEN. Appreciate that.

Secretary HAGEL. But, I think that maybe there are some areas that we could do a little better with, as far as in dealing with families and the human part of this. And again, that's not meant as criticism for any of our agencies or departments, because I don't know all the facts on how it was handled.

Senator SHAHEEN. Well, I certainly——

General DEMPSEY. Senator, could I just——

Senator SHAHEEN. Sure.

General DEMPSEY.—just because you mentioned the mission, itself. I've been at this a long time. That was the most complex, highest-risk mission we've ever undertaken. And that should give the families some solace and you some confidence that, as a military, we are very focused on this. We had—we have some limitations in our ability to collect intelligence inside of Syria. But, when we had the opportunity to do so, we tried to get them.

Senator SHAHEEN. And I appreciate that. I do hope, though, given what we've heard from the Foleys and from the other families, that there will be a reassessment of how our government supports families facing this kind of a crisis.

I want to go, next, to the estimate of ISIL's troop strengthen, because it's been—you—as you reported, 31,000 is the most recent estimate. How could it have grown to that size without our intelligence recognizing the threat? And what is part of our plan to address the recruitment? There have been a lot of reports about how effective the messaging is that ISIL has been using to recruit young people, particularly Westerners. So, how is that part of our plan? And why is our intelligence not picking up the extent to which this effort has been growing?

General DEMPSEY. I can't speak for the Intelligence Committee or the intelligence agencies. I'll tell you they're focused on it. The way they grow, though—I mentioned that——

Senator SHAHEEN. Right.

General DEMPSEY.—that ISIL's strategy is actually to consume tribes. And so, they may be in a conflict with a tribe one day, and then overcome it the next, which might increase their numbers by 3-, 4-, 5,000. Once the tribal leader pledges allegiance, the entire thing shifts over.

So, that's part of it, I think. Other—they've also sprung a few thousand prisoners from different prisons inside of Iraq that are—that were very hardened terrorists.

So, they are growing. But, again, the numbers that are reported are—were estimated based on the free rein that, at the time, ISIL was having in Iraq. I think we're going to see some shift in that. That's part of our strategy, actually. And the public diplomacy part of this, which is not a military line of effort, but it has to be a—it has to be part of our strategy. We have to point out to Arab and Muslim youth—and Western youth, for that matter—the risk posed by this ideology.

Senator SHAHEEN. Well, thank you. My time is up, but I just want to close by saying I'd—I certainly intend to support the request for funding to train and equip vetted opposition groups in Syria. But, I do believe that it would be a mistake for us not, in Congress, to have a debate about a long-term, broader strategy to go after ISIL. I think it's very important for us to have a bipartisan, bicameral support for that effort and a debate here that the American people can be part of. So, I certainly—I know that the Chairman of the Foreign Relations Committee is working on a specific authorization for use of military force, which I intend to work with him on. And I certainly hope there will be an effort on the part of the administration to work with Congress on that.

Thank you, Mr. Chairman.

Chairman LEVIN. Thank you, Senator Shaheen.

Senator Lee.

Senator LEE. Thank you, Mr. Chairman.

Thanks, to both of you, for being here today and for all you do for our country and all you do to keep us safe. This is an exceptionally important issue as it relates to our national security.

I think the President, last week, quite accurately portrayed the threats that we're facing from ISIS, that it's a threat to the Middle East with aspirations to attack global targets, including the United States. The President should, in my opinion, do everything he possibly can to protect Americans and to protect U.S. facilities in Iraq and Syria from ISIS and from other terrorist activity.

I believe, however, like many of my colleagues on both sides of the aisle, that the President should seek congressional authorization for his expanded campaign to degrade and destroy ISIS. I also do not believe that we should authorize parts of this conflict through a continuing resolution. This is a serious and important discussion about our National security, and it should be debated and discussed and ultimately voted on within Congress, based on its own merits, and it shouldn't be lumped in with a much broader discussion about a lot of other things. I think we owe it to those who valiantly put their own lives on the line, to make sure that this is debated and discussed, and that the parameters are properly set in its own context.

Secretary Hagel, I've got a question for you as it relates to some of this discussion as it relates to some of the things that President Obama has said in recent weeks about ISIS. In an interview that he gave to—I believe it was with Thomas Friedman at the New York Times, just barely a month ago, he stated that the notion of arming Syrian rebels has—and the next few sentences are all in a quote—has, quote, "always been a fantasy. This idea that we could provide some light arms or even sophisticated arms to what was essentially an opposition made up of former doctors, farmers, pharmacists, and so forth, and that they were going to be able to be able to battle not only a well-armed state, but also a well-armed state backed by Russia, backed by Iran, a battle-hardened Hezbollah, that was never in the cards," close quote.

Now, the President, hardly a month later, is seeking authorization to do basically that. So, Mr. Secretary, what has changed? And why does the President, who apparently didn't think that would work, and described that as some sort of fantasy about a month—what has changed to make him think that it will work now?

Secretary HAGEL. Well, first—thank you, Senator—at the risk of interpreting what the President meant when he said that, I recognize that is always risky, as I have said. But, let me address your question this way.

What's changed now is the urgency in—of what has occurred in the Middle East, specifically in Iraq and Syria, the murder of two Americans, now a third, a brutal murder of a British citizen, the different dimensions that we've seen, the last 5 weeks especially, unfold, what ISIL has been able to achieve in a relatively short amount of time, the changing of a government, the leaving of one Iraqi government with a new government coming in. Over about a 6-week period, Senator, there was, and were, a number of occurrences that came together that I do think presented a whole new picture of realities, of urgency, of dangers, of threats. So, let me stop there and see if that helps you a little bit.

I saw the interview, and I read the interview. But, again, at the risk of trying to interpret what he meant, I offer that.

Senator LEE. Yes. No, I—and I appreciate that. And I do understand that things—that there were some developments have—that have occurred since then that have brought this appropriately to our attention, to the attention of the world. I would be curious to know, though, strategically, how that changes what—how that changes something that he previously described as a kind of fantasy into something that could be realistic. But, I understand that that's difficult for you to answer in this context. I'd love to be able to talk more about that on another occasion if we can.

Can you describe what the end objective in Syria is for the United States? In other words, do we still contend that Assad must go, that he cannot stay in power, and also that the—what the objective is as it relates to the moderate groups that we would like—that the President would like to see lead this—what does the post-Assad Syria look like that we are after? Or is that our objective at all?

Secretary HAGEL. The issue on our position with Assad remains very clear. The President stated it, I said it in my testimony here this morning. The President has said, many times, still strongly believes, that Assad has lost the legitimacy to govern his own people. We've got a country, Syria, in complete chaos and upheaval because of Assad. That's the individual responsible for creating what is occurring and has been occurring.

Your question about the end state in Syria. I think what we, the administration, I think the American people, would want to see—and I hope the—and believe—the Syrian people—is a free Syria, where men and women and their families have rights to choose and have rights to determine their own leaders and their own futures. And I think that's—is really the essence of the ultimate objective we'd like to see in Syria.

Senator LEE. Okay. I see my time is expired. Thank you, Mr. Secretary.

Secretary HAGEL. Senator, thank you.

Chairman LEVIN. Thank you, Senator Lee.

Senator Blumenthal.

Senator BLUMENTHAL. Thank you, Mr. Chairman.

Thank you, to both Secretary Hagel and Chairman Dempsey, for again being with us and for your explanation and very forthright testimony here today and, in the past, both publicly and privately, to members of this committee and the Senate.

I want to quote to you—I want to say to you, first, Secretary Hagel, how much I appreciate the decision that you made recently to change the Department of Defense policy on reviewing other-than-honorable discharges for veterans suffering, at the time of their discharge, from post-traumatic stress, and most especially, my thanks to you on behalf of the 80,000 Vietnam-era veterans who will benefit by that policy change to give them liberal consideration as they apply to the discharge review boards. These veterans who suffered, at the time of their discharge, from post-traumatic stress often received less-than-honorable discharges because of the injuries that they suffered in combat, at war. And they've lived with the stigma and the blackmark on their records for decades, many of them became homeless and jobless as a result. And I want to thank you for committing to me, when we first met, that you would do the right thing, and then, in fact, doing the right thing. So, I really appreciate your policy change in that regard.

And I want to, perhaps unfairly, quote to you something that you said on the floor of the Senate in 2002, in October, at the time that the Senate voted in favor, and you voted in favor, of Senate Joint

Resolution 45, which was the resolution that authorized the use of force in Iraq. You said, "In authorizing"—I'm quoting—"the use of force against Iraq, we are at the beginning of a road that has no clear end." And you went on to say, "While I cannot predict the future, I believe that what we decide in this chamber this week will influence America's security and role in the world for the coming decades. It will serve as the framework, both intentionally and unintentionally, for the future"—and then you said, quite wisely, in my view, as it turns out—"for an intensification of engagement with Iraq in the Middle East, a world which we know very little and whose destiny will now be directly tied to ours."

We've lived with the framework that came from that vote. We've suffered, as Americans, greatly in both the loss of people and the sacrifice of treasure, money. And that is the reason why Americans now feel so conflicted, often ambivalent, about the brutality of the action that we've witnessed—the beheading, shockingly, repulsively, of these two brave individuals—and yet, the war weariness that many Americans feel at this point.

General Dempsey mentioned earlier the quote from Thomas Friedman, that nobody ever washed a used car. But, a lot of people have rented unwashed cars. And it seems to me we are, in effect, renting an unwashed car, insofar as we want to make sure that it's serviceable and it works, but do not want to go into a situation where there's no clearly defined exit strategy.

Can you tell us what the threat is to the United States that we will eliminate by degrading and defeating ISIL?

Secretary HAGEL. Well, that's always the problem of giving a speech on the floor of the Senate. [Laughter.]

That it is on the record.

Let me just comment on that, because it is going to reflect on my answer to your question.

I put a lot of time into thinking about that speech, Senator, and I recall writing it. And what—part of it that you read back, I do not disassociate myself from at all. For those words that you read back, I'm even more mindful, as Secretary of Defense, of my responsibilities. Doesn't mean I'm right, but I'm even more mindful than I might otherwise be of what I saw occur, starting in 2001–2002, and I was part of. That's first.

Second, to the real question, What is the threat, and how will it change? I think we are in a different situation today, in what the President has laid out to the American people as to what his objectives are, versus where we were in 2002. Main reason is that ISIL is a very clear threat to the United States of America, to our people. You mentioned the two brutal murders of two Americans. That's not just a threat, that's an action that was taken.

There are a number of other examples. To our allies. I thought General Dempsey's commentary to answer a question—a difficult question of—Senator Manchin posed—was full of a lot of thoughtful and wise thinking on where this is all going to go if we don't do what we should do and need to do now. I think that's different from where we were in 2002.

Now, because I do think it—ISIL is a threat, and a very clear threat, to the United States, to our interests, to our people, to our allies—and we could spend a lot more time this morning going through that case and making that case—I think what the President's laid out, what I strongly support, is the right thing to do, because it is in the interest, clearly, of our country.

One last point on this. What General Dempsey said about "If we don't do something now"—and I think the way the President has framed that "something," how we're going to do it—we can't do it alone. And I think it's been clear in a lot of the testimony this morning, in the questions, that this country, the United States of America, as much as we have engaged, as much as we have bled, the treasure and the lives that we have left behind, we still haven't fixed the problem. One—we can't fix the problem alone. And that's why all the dimensions of what the President's talking about, to me, make sense. And I think if we can do what we intend to do and what we believe we can do, bringing all these groups together, the very people who are most at risk, then we can be successful at averting this great threat to this country. That's what's different. That's what I think the threat is.

Chairman LEVIN. Thank you.

Senator BLUMENTHAL. Thank you.

Chairman LEVIN. Thank you, Senator Blumenthal.

Senator Cruz.

Senator CRUZ. Thank you, Mr. Chairman.

Gentlemen, thank you for being here today. Thank you for your service, especially during these challenging times.

Mr. Secretary, I want to start with you, asking—If ISIS is able to consolidate power and to create and dominate a nation-state and to retain access to, potentially, billions of dollars in oil revenue, over time what is the specific danger to America if they are able to use that nation-state to project jihad here?

Secretary HAGEL. Senator, as you have expressed it and asked the question, over time if ISIL is not stopped—and you've mentioned the economic power that it has now—then what I would foresee happening, not only immediately threat to United States citizens and our people, our interests, but I think you could very well find Jordan go down as a—as the country that we know it today. I think Saudi Arabia could well be beyond just threatened, their oilfields. I think the expansion of where this could go in the Middle East, dominating oil production. Lebanon is also in a very tentative state. Libya is in chaos. Everywhere you look in the Middle East, there is trouble. And if a force like ISIL, in my opinion, is allowed to continue with its ideology, with its resources, with its capability, then, as General Dempsey said, there's no doubt, it will impact this country and the world economy. It—now, this is down the road, if this is not stopped. But, I think that's what we're looking at here, Senator. It—but, it's an immediate threat to our interests, as well.

Senator CRUZ. General Dempsey, worst-case scenario, if ISIS were allowed to consolidate power, in your judgment what would be the worst-case specific risk to the homeland and to the lives of American citizens?

General DEMPSEY. Yes, Senator. The combination of radical ideology plus a youth bulge—the entire region is suffering a youth bulge—inequitable distribution of resources and a state of Islamic radicalization would, first of all, almost surely trigger a confrontation with Iran into which the rest of the world would be drawn, for obvious reason, but also provides them with this combination of resources plus radical ideology that we actually haven't seen. Most of the radical ideologies are resource-starved, or at least resource-limited. A resource-rich radical ideology must become a threat. It's just inconceivable that it wouldn't be.

Senator CRUZ. Do you believe, if they were able to consolidate that power, that there would be a risk of their attempting, and perhaps even succeeding, with a terrorist attack of the magnitude of that that occurred on September 11th, 2001, or potentially an even greater terrorist attack?

General DEMPSEY. I'd phrase it this way. Given what they've already demonstrated, in terms of brutality and utter disregard for human life, other than that which adheres to their ideology, whatever weapon system they would have in their possession, there's no doubt in my mind they'd use it, to include weapons of mass destruction.

Senator CRUZ. Well, and let me ask about—it's been reported that upwards of 100 Americans are fighting alongside ISIS, have affiliated themselves with ISIS. How would you assess the risk of Americans with U.S. passports coming back to the United States to carry out acts of terror here?

General DEMPSEY. Yes, we've actually been in close contact with both the intelligence communities and law enforcement. And the risk will increase unless their momentum is reversed and unless their dominance of the media space—they are actually quite capable in social media and other forms of messaging. So, unless their momentum is blunted, which will begin to strip away this myth that they've surrounded themselves with, and unless we counter them in the media space, then the risk of radicalization through things like the Internet will continue to rise.

Senator CRUZ. But, you would characterize the risks of Americans coming back from ISIS with U.S. passports as significant? Is that fair?

General DEMPSEY. I do. And that view is shared by our European allies, as well.

Senator CRUZ. If the objective were to destroy ISIS—not to just degrade them, but to destroy them within 90 days, what would be required militarily to carry that out?

General DEMPSEY. It's not possible, Senator, because—militarily, we could confront them, we could destroy a lot of equipment, we could drive them underground, if you will. But, as I said, they will only be defeated or destroyed once they're rejected by the populations in which they hide. I mean, there is no—truly, there is no military solution to ISIL.

Senator CRUZ. What would be required to kill those who are taking up arms right now?

General DEMPSEY. Well, actually, I think that's the path we're on, which is to say using our unique capabilities, our counterterror capabilities, our ISR capabilities, our air capabilities, while working on the rest of the equation, which is this coalition of willing allied partners, or willing Arab partners. There is no—I mean, it may be a tough pill to swallow, but there is no military solution. It's go to be part of a broader whole-of-government regional campaign.

Senator CRUZ. And one final question, Secretary Hagel. The President, as I understand it, has laid out what could be an extended military operation that could extend many months, or even years. In my view, carrying out such an operation, not responding to immediate exigency, requires congressional authorization. And I think Congress would be prepared to grant that authorization if a specific case were made with clear objectives. What is your position as to the legal authority of the administration to carry out an extended military campaign for years, potentially, absent congressional authorization?

Secretary HAGEL. Well, I believe the President has the statutory and constitutional authority to take the action that he is doing to protect this country as he laid it out to the American people last week.

Senator CRUZ. And what is the legal authority that you're basing that on?

Secretary HAGEL. Well, the statutory authority is the AUMF of 2001, and I think you—if you wanted to add something to that, it would probably be the AUMF of 2003.

Senator CRUZ. My time is expired.

Chairman LEVIN. Thank you.

I assume that you meant there's no purely military solution to ISIL. And when you said there's no military—because you're seeking——

General DEMPSEY. Yes, there's no——

Chairman LEVIN. Okay.

General DEMPSEY.—purely military solution.

Chairman LEVIN. Thank you.

General DEMPSEY. Right.

Chairman LEVIN. Thank you.

Now, we're going to need to stick very carefully to the 6-minute rule, because we have—one, two, three, four, five, at least. And so, we have to be out of here at exactly 1 p.m. So, please, watch that clock, everybody.

Senator DONNELLY. I'm not your problem. [Laughter.]

Chairman LEVIN. Senator Donnelly. I didn't mean to——

Senator DONNELLY. No, no, I know that. I know that, Mr. Chairman. Thank you.

I want to thank both of you for everything you've done and for your service to our country.

And I want to get back to what you were talking about as to having to have partners and to have buy-in. And I've heard the role that John Allen is going to play. And is a big part of that role, in your minds, working with the Sunni tribal leadership, the people they've worked with before, to try to get them to get back to a place almost that they were before, which is working together with us and, in effect, almost a second Awakening?

General DEMPSEY. Yes, that's one of the reasons John was such a attractive figure for that role. You know, Lloyd Austin, the Commander of CENTCOM, has great—you know, he was in Iraq, as well—he's got a relationship, he's got incredible regional relationships, though this coalition will be beyond the region. We're looking for European partners, and maybe even nontraditional partners. But, John Allen is certainly going to focus on the tribes.

Senator DONNELLY. And General Austin has done a tremendous job, but it doesn't hurt to have someone else in the lineup to help him with it, I would think. And when we look at this, what are the kind of things that General Allen can do, in effect, to start to get the tribes to look at this differently, to say, "Look, our interests are more aligned with this coalition that's being put together than with this group, ISIS"?

General DEMPSEY. Well, at the National level, I think he will, along with our diplomats, encourage the new Iraqi government to answer some of the grievances that both the Sunnis and the Kurds have had for years, actually, since 2004. And I think there's some indication that there's reason to believe that that could occur.

The Sunni tribes in al-Anbar aspire to form a national guard—have for some time. And I think that's one of the capabilities that might actually contribute significantly to that outcome. The Maliki government was actually, as you might expect them to be, very much against the idea of a national guard in al-Anbar, believing they were already dealing with a national guard of sorts in the Peshmerga in Kurdistan. But, I think this government may be more open to it, and I think that'll be one of the lines of effort.

Senator DONNELLY. Is this something—and this is for either of you—that we can get done in Iraq if we don't get buy-in from the Sunnis?

General DEMPSEY. As I said at a—in an earlier question, Senator, every campaign plan makes assumptions, and then, if those assumptions are valid, you stay on path; if the assumption is rendered invalid, you deviate. One of the really important assumptions of this campaign is that we can, in fact, separate the moderate Sunni tribes from the ISIL ideology. If that proves untrue, we've got to go back to the drawing board.

Senator DONNELLY. Okay. And, you know, you had talked before about taking back Mosul, and the effort to do that. And it would involve ISF, in that we're working with the best parts of ISF, or trying to. And I guess this touches back again on that same subject, which is getting the Sunnis to accept those parts of ISF. Is that part of what General Allen is going to do, and what General Austin is working on?

General DEMPSEY. Absolutely, yes, sir.

Senator DONNELLY. Okay. And this is, again, for either of you. There are reports that you mentioned, financially, about ISIS, you know, getting income of $3 to $5 million per day, is what we've heard, that they are the best-financed terrorist group. So many of them have tried to put shoelaces and chewing gum together. That's not the case here. And so, what is the plan, or what are we working on, to try to cut off their financing? Because the oil they're selling has to be going somewhere, and someone has to be paying them. So, how are we going to do that?

Secretary HAGEL. Senator, I mentioned this in two previous answers here.

Senator DONNELLY. And I apologize, I wasn't here for that.

Secretary HAGEL. But, it's an important question. And I also noted it in my testimony, that the administration has put together a focus, working with our Treasury Department as the key interagency department, with all other allies and partners around the world. You mentioned oil, the black marketing of oil—they've—is—has been, recently, a very significant resource——

Senator DONNELLY. Right.

Secretary HAGEL.—for them. They have taken small oilfields in Syria and Iraq. That's something that we can address through what we're looking at on some of our strategic focus outside of the Treasury Department. The ransom, the terrorism, all of the ways they finance themselves, we have a task force, working through the Treasury Department, to focus on this. But, that has to be, and is, a major part of our overall strategy, to cut off that funding and flow of resources.

Senator DONNELLY. And the last thing I'll ask is about coordination with our European allies in regards to the people with European passports who can get visa waivers and other things, the efforts that are going into that. Is that being done with all of our European allies over there? And what coordination is being——

Secretary HAGEL. That, too, is a major part of the coordination, not only with our allies, but it is part of the overall strategic focus of our interagency departments, and we are working on all that. And that's law enforcement, that's State Department, it's all the other agencies coming together to focus on it. We took it up, by the way, at Wales, at the NATO Summit, 2 weeks ago, when we were together, as we will continue to do. But, it's a very significant part of the overall strategy.

Senator DONNELLY. Thank you both.

Thank you, Mr. Chairman.

Chairman LEVIN. Thank you, Senator Donnelly.

Senator Sessions.

Senator SESSIONS. Thank you, gentlemen, both for your service and—we're dealing with some difficult times.

But, General Dempsey, you served in combat in Iraq, you served as a—you were in charge of training the Iraqi troops. How many years ago was that?

General DEMPSEY. 2005 to 2007, sir.

Senator SESSIONS. So, that's several years we've been training the Iraqi troops. Will they fight?

General DEMPSEY. Yes, they will fight, if they are well led and believe that their government is looking out for, not only their best interests, but their families.

Senator SESSIONS. Will they—is it—will they be encouraged if they felt they had United States air support?

General DEMPSEY. Absolutely.

Senator SESSIONS. Well, I believe you said earlier that our first priority should be ISIL. Is that correct?

General DEMPSEY. I did, Senator.

Senator SESSIONS. And I agree with that. There's no doubt about that in my mind. Don't we have a commitment, to the Kurds, the Shi'a, the Sunnis that we worked with for 10 years in war and helped them establish, at least for a time, a government that functioned in Iraq—don't we have, as a nation, some sort of relationship, a bond between our two nations, even though we've had difficulties in recent years?

General DEMPSEY. Well, I can tell you that those who have, sort of, served there obviously feel that bond.

Senator SESSIONS. I certainly hear that from people who have served there. And I think we owe those who have served and who have suffered to be successful, if we can be successful. And I think we can be successful.

Now, we've had a lot of questions about Syria. And there are many complications in Syria. But, if we're going to make ISIL the first priority, shouldn't we make that—shouldn't we emphasize our relationship with our friends, the Kurds, in Baghdad, and the Iraqis, and begin to work with them to turn the tide? Isn't that—in terms of strategy, where you begin, wouldn't the first place to be to push—put ISIL on the defensive in our ally, Iraq?

General DEMPSEY. Yes.

Senator SESSIONS. Well, I'm a little—would embedding troops—I want your military opinion—but, if we embedded a number of Special Forces with the Iraqi military, and they knew that they had access to intelligence from the United States and air support from the United States, wouldn't that encourage them to be more effective, militarily?

General DEMPSEY. As I mentioned in my opening statement, the—there may be times when I believe that would be necessary in order to make the mission successful. I don't think so on a day-to-day basis.

Senator SESSIONS. Well, let me just ask you directly. If there's a military unit in Iraq today, an Iraqi unit, and they had United States military embedded with them, and they were asked to undertake an offensive operation, would they not be more emboldened and encouraged to know that they had Americans there with them?

General DEMPSEY. Well, in those cases where I would assess the mission to be complex enough that it would absolutely require our expertise forward, I will—we'll—I'll make a recommendation to do it. We also don't want them to become dependent upon us. And there's a fine line to be drawn there.

Senator SESSIONS. Well, they've become a bit dependent on U.S. air, I acknowledge. But, I do believe you're correct, that they will fight. But, they do need—I don't think they will have the kind of morale boost that we'd like them to have if they don't have confidence that they have air support, and that is enhanced with embedded soldiers. Surely, that's true, is it not?

General DEMPSEY. Well, I'm actually eager—I would love to find an occasion where we might have Jordanian Special Forces embedded, and Emirati——

Senator SESSIONS. Well, if we all——

General DEMPSEY.—Special Forces embedded——

Senator SESSIONS.—had horses, we'd take a ride. We don't have that. And that's all——

General DEMPSEY. Yes, sir.

Senator SESSIONS. We're talking about down the road. So, you said, several times, we need to blunt the momentum, we need to change the momentum on the battlefield. Don't we need to start taking back a territory in Iraq—those of us who share that view——

General DEMPSEY. Yes, absolutely, Senator.

Senator SESSIONS.—and can't we get——

General DEMPSEY. But, your premise is that we have to have U.S. embedded advisors forward. That—and I don't share that premise, at this point.

Senator SESSIONS. Did we use embedded people when they took the Haditha Dam back?

General DEMPSEY. We did not.

Senator SESSIONS. How did we assist them in that instance?

General DEMPSEY. We have advisors embedded in headquarters that can help direct, using overhead imagery, full-motion video, and direct strikes.

Senator SESSIONS. Well, would it be in our advantage to, sooner rather than later, encourage the Iraqis to get on the move?

General DEMPSEY. Absolutely. But, we want to make sure they're ready, as well.

Senator SESSIONS. How long is it—well, you started training them in 2007, and it's been a number of months now, and we've had only—I just think we're in a position to start taking some advances. I think it's necessary and—to blunt the momentum.

Secretary Hagel, briefly, I notice that the House put in the—their CR, 91 billion for the OCO funding. And the President had asked for 58-. Is that money going to be used to—in addition to the 550 million for training and equipping the Syrian—Free Syrian Army? Is that going to be used for—carry out military operations in the region?

Secretary HAGEL. Well, I haven't seen what the House did, and I think our comptroller may be here. If I might take a second to ask Mike McCord, who you all know, Mr. Chairman——

Chairman LEVIN. Have to make it real quick, because we have four more——

Secretary HAGEL. Okay, because I haven't seen the—I haven't seen what the House did. And I don't want to say and—or respond to that until I know——

Senator SESSIONS. Could you respond in writing——

Secretary HAGEL. We can do that.

Senator SESSIONS.—on what your position is——

Secretary HAGEL. We can do it for the record.

Senator SESSIONS.—with regard to this?

Thank you, Mr. Chairman.

Chairman LEVIN. Thank you.

Secretary HAGEL. We could—I'll provide it for the record.

Chairman LEVIN. And if we could get that this afternoon. Because, obviously, it's important what the administration's——

Secretary HAGEL. We will.

[The information referred to follows:]

[INFORMATION]

Chairman LEVIN.—position is.

Senator Hirono.

Senator HIRONO. Thank you, Mr. Chairman.

And thank both of you for your service.

You and the President have made a very strong case that ISIL, if left unchecked, will be a threat to Europe and to the United States. And they are attracting recruits from all over the world, including the United States.

General Dempsey, you noted that, as we were looking at that map, what looks like territorial gains by ISIL is really a tribal-by-tribal overcoming. So, my question to you, General Dempsey, is, How important is it—even as we are asked to provide the authorization to arm and equip the Free Syrian Army, how important is it that we work with the Sunni tribal leaders to enable them to fight off ISIL in both Syria and Iraq?

General DEMPSEY. It's absolutely an integral part of the campaign plan.

Senator HIRONO. So, what, exactly, are we doing working with the Sunni tribal leaders to enable them to fend off ISIL?

General DEMPSEY. The—this is a—probably requires the integration of several things. I mentioned, already, the fact that the Iraqi government has to demonstrate that it actually cares about the Sunni tribes and not to just fence them off in al-Anbar Province. That's one line of effort. The other is the effort of John Allen, as he goes forward using some of his previous relationships to meet with the tribal leaders and begin the formation of a national guard for al-Anbar Province. And then, I think it'll be a matter of regional partners who have Sunni governments providing some of the—maybe most, actually—of the funding and materiel support to that organization.

Senator HIRONO. Do you see evidence that this kind of effort is working, that these tribal leaders that have been marginalized or excluded are now going to trust what we're doing?

General DEMPSEY. I can't make that report yet, Senator. What I will tell you is that, while ISIL was making these broad, sweeping movements across Iraq, many of the Sunni tribes completely got discouraged and wanted to be—for what was going to happen—they didn't want to—they didn't feel like they had any reason or capability to stand up to ISIL.

Now that ISIL has been—the momentum has been slowed, it hasn't been stopped and it hasn't been reversed, but it's been slowed—and we did see, today, actually, an ISF unit moving south of Baghdad, near Jurf al-Sakhar, for the first movement south of Baghdad. Now all of a sudden we're getting tribal leaders reaching out, saying, "Okay, if you're going to be serious about this, then we'll talk to you."

So, I think it was a necessary first step that we showed them we were—really were serious.

Senator HIRONO. There were some earlier questions about concerns being raised about the Free Syrian Army that has been fighting Assad. And what makes us believe that, when we train and equip them, that they will turn their attention to fighting ISIL? Do we have some kind of an agreement with the 5,000 forces—Syrian army forces that we are going to vet and train that—do we have some kind of an agreement that says, "You will fight ISIL and you're not going to be fighting Assad"?

General DEMPSEY. No. We do not have any agreements at all, because we haven't begun the recruiting effort. We haven't—we don't have the authority to begin, so we haven't really done anything but come up with a concept.

Senator HIRONO. Let's say that you do get the authority. Then what kind of terms would you put forth to enable us, as much as possible—we realize there are risks, here—to have us conclude that the people we are recruiting are actually going to fight ISIL and not Assad?

General DEMPSEY. Well, the important part of an overt program is, we'll actually —as—we'll link it to a political structure over which we will have a certain amount of influence because of their dependence upon us for supplies, ammunition, and so forth—as well as the fact that the regional partners, in particular, I think, as long as they're—if the regional partners believe we're just going to ignore Assad and just leave him there in perpetuity, then we're going to have a problem with building a coalition. But, we can, it seems to me, coalesce around the idea that ISIL is the immediate threat and, therefore, should be addressed first.

Senator HIRONO. And, of course, there is the question of, What is Assad going to be doing while the Free Syrian Army is busy attacking ISIL? There are a lot of complexities——

General DEMPSEY. There are.

Senator HIRONO.—involving Syria.

Secretary Hagel, we know that ISIL is attracting recruits from all over the world, including from the United States. And I note, in your testimony, that you said that the Department of Justice, Department of Homeland Security have launched an initiative to partner with local communities to counter extremist recruiting. Can you talk a little bit more about what this constitutes, what this initiative is all about?

Secretary HAGEL. First, thank you for pointing that out, because it's—as I noted in one of my earlier answers, it's a very important component of the overall strategy here to deal with ISIL. Since I'm not involved in that part of the strategy and the operations, I can't go too deep into how they're doing it, exactly. But, the point being is to enlist local communities' law enforcement awareness of who's in their communities, who's coming in and out of their communities, just be more alert of things that are out there that will help our homeland security people, our law enforcement individuals be more aware of things that are—may be occurring, shouldn't occur, and then also working with our international partners as we trade information on individuals who are flowing in and out of these countries. We know, as you have mentioned, and I think Marty mentioned and I mentioned, that there are thousands of Europeans that we know are in Syria and the Middle East, and these people all have passports which allow them access to our country, to different countries in the world. So, it's a combination of using those sources and coordinating that effort.

Chairman LEVIN. Thank you, Senator Hirono.

Senator HIRONO. Thank you.

Chairman LEVIN. Senator Kaine.

Senator KAINE. Thank you, Mr. Chairman.

And thank you, to the witnesses, for your helpful testimony today.

I believe the President's four-pillar plan, announced last Wednesday night, is generally reasonable, but I have one significant point of disagreement that I want to spend some time on, and that is the question of whether the President has the authority, without additional congressional authorization, to carry out the mission, as described.

Secretary Hagel, you have used the phrase "war against ISIL" today, and others in the administration have used that phrase. And, General Dempsey, you have talked about a multiyear effort, and others of—in the administration have expressed the same concern. And I believe very strongly—and I don't think that it's just a theoretical or law-professor argument, that the President does need the authority of Congress to conduct the mission that he described and you've discussed today.

The President's power is basically—in a matter like this, is composed of two kinds of powers—and you've alluded to them—constitutional or statutory. The constitutional power is under Article 2, as powers Commander in Chief. While there's some gray area that's been debated often since 1787, the general understanding of the power of a Commander in Chief under Article 2 is to defend the Nation. An offensive military action then triggers the need to go into Article 1 and have Congress declare war. That was first tested by a Virginia President, Thomas Jefferson, when fighting a terrorist organization of his day in the same general region, the Barbary pirates. He had the authority, and believed he did, to repel attacks, one after the next. But, when he decided he need to go on offense, "Well, let's wipe out this threat so we don't have to just keep repelling attacks," he stated plainly that, "I can't do that. I can't go on offense without Congress."

Senator Obama said a—made the same point very clearly in 2007, "The President does not have power under the Constitution to unilaterally authorize a military attack in a situation that does not involve stopping an actual ongoing or imminent threat against the Nation." Within the last 2 weeks, the head of—the Director of National Counterterrorism Center, Matthew Olson, said, "At this point, there is no credible information that ISIL is planning to attack the United States." I understood the President's comments last week, and other comments, to suggest that ISIL is a significant threat, a serious threat, a growing threat, but, in terms of an imminent threat to attack the United States that would trigger the Article 2 defense powers, it does not seem to exist at this point.

Then there are statutory powers. And the White House has cited both the 2001 and 2002 AUMFs. 2001 AUMF, it's important to remember not only what Congress authorized, but what Congress refused to authorize. The Bush administration approached Congress and said, "We would like the power to undertake military action against terrorist groups in order to prevent terrorist attacks on the United States." If Congress had granted that AUMF, it clearly would have covered this threat. But, Congress overwhelmingly rejected that wording of the AUMF, did not believe in a preemptive war doctrine, did not want to hand the power to an executive to unilaterally determine who to go after. Instead, Congress narrowed the AUMF to have it be with respect to the perpetrators of the attacks of September 11. ISIL was formed after September 11. There's been an administrative gloss by both administrations, the Bush and Obama administration, to go beyond the perpetrators of September 11 to talk about associated forces with al Qaeda. Has there been a time which ISIL has been associated with al-Qaeda?

There was a time. But, they are not associated now. They've disclaimed each other. They're even battling in some theaters.

Could a lawyer make a broad argument, a really creative argument the—that the ONAUMF covered ISIL? I suppose. I'm a lawyer, I've made creative arguments. But, this President spoke at the National Defense University in May 2013, and he argued against broadening the open-ended AUMF and said, instead, what we should be doing as a Nation, and what he was committed to, was not broadening the open-ended AUMF, but trying to refine it, narrow it, and ultimately repeal it. I don't know why we would take an open-ended AUMF and try to broaden it further when the President has made a commitment that it should be narrowed and refined.

Finally, there was the AUMF with respect to Iraq that was passed in 2002. It was designed to topple a government that is long gone. There have been many successive governments since the Hussein government was toppled. I think—and the administration testified, in a Foreign Relations Committee hearing here in May, that the 2002 AUMF was obsolete and should be repealed. Again, to try to take these two statutory elements and stretch them so broadly, I think is a significant problem, and it will create a precedent that, if we go along with it in Congress, we will live to regret, and possibly regret very soon.

That said, I think the mission, as described, is reasonable. But, I think Congress is necessary. And the President, last week, and you, today, have said, obviously, you would welcome Congress, because we're stronger if we do it together, not just as an institution. We're stronger in the support we provide to the men and women that we ask to bear the risk of battle. If we ask them to bear the risk of battle in a war that may take a number of years, that will have aspects that we can't currently predict, some will be hurt, some will lose their lives, some will see bad things happen to their comrades in arms. If we're going to ask them to risk that, then we should do our job to bless the mission and say that it's worth it. And if we're not willing to do our job as Congress, bless the mission and say that it's worth it, we shouldn't be asking people to risk everything.

It is my hope that this body will grapple with this four-point plan, will ask tough questions, will refine it, but will give our imprimatur to it so that we are not asking men and women to serve and potentially risk everything without us doing the job that we're supposed to do in order to demonstrate the National support for the mission that we're asking them to carry out.

Thank you, Mr. Chairman.

Chairman LEVIN. Thank you very much, Senator Kaine.

Senator King.

Senator KING. I'm in complete agreement with Senator Kaine, and I'm glad he went before me, because he articulated it much more clearly and forcefully than I would have.

I would only touch a bit on the history. The Constitution is very clear, and it wasn't an afterthought or a minor comma here or there, "Congress shall declare war." In fact, the interesting thing is, the first draft of the Constitution said, "Congress shall make war." And they had an—they argued about an amendment to change "make" to "declare," because they realized it was impractical for Congress to execute the war, so they changed it to "declare" to leave the power of execution to the President. But, they were very explicit about why they did that. If you look at the 69th Federalist, it talks about the differences between the President and the King or other executives—and this is one of the principal things they pointed to—and the risk of having the power of war exclusively vested in the executive.

In Madison's notes to the Constitution on—I think it's August 17th, 1787—Madison talks about this discussion of the declaration of war, and George Mason used a wonderful phrase. He said, "It is our intention—it is our goal—our goal here is clogging rather than facilitating war." That's an interesting term. They wanted it to be a deliberate decision.

And I believe, along with Senator Kaine, that stretching the AUMF from 2001 or 2002 to cover this situation renders the constitutional clause a nullity. And I just believe, both for—and the danger here is, as this happens year by year, war by war, conflict by conflict, eventually there's nothing left of that provision, and we have, in fact, transferred to the executive the unilateral power to commit American forces. That's not good for this country, and they're going to—there may—we may like this President. There may be a President down the road we don't like and we don't want to have this power. And the more precedent we establish—and it started with Harry Truman in Korea, where there was no declaration—I think the more—the stronger that precedent becomes embedded, the more dangerous it is for the country.

And I think it's significant that the administration is now using the word "war." I won't go further, but I think it's an important point. And I totally agree that Congress has to act, and it's our responsibility to act. It's our responsibility to act. And it will strengthen the President's hand, it will strengthen the coalition, it will strengthen our ability to draw coalition partners if we are a unified country and we're not—Congress isn't doing what it usually does, which is criticize and second-guess, and instead is a participant in the decision.

Second point. We need to be thinking about three levels of strategy here, it seems to me. One is the plan the President articulated, which I believe was a coherent, thoughtful, and strong position. The President has articulated a plan. The question is, as General Dempsey has alluded to today, what if we do—what do we do—what's Plan B if the coalition doesn't stand up? What do—what happens if Turkey and Saudi Arabia or all the other countries decide that they're just not going to participate, and then we're in a position of the West waging war on Islam?—which is exactly what ISIL wants. We cannot—cannot be in that position. We've already quoted Tom Friedman today. I would—I'll do it again. He had a wonderful phrase, and I'd apply it—paraphrase it applying to Turkey. "They're with us on Monday, Wednesday, and Friday. They're against us on Tuesday and Thursday. And they take the weekends off." These other countries have to get engaged in this struggle. Turkey is one of the prime candidates, because that's the jihadi interstate, that's how the people are getting into Syria and getting to ISIL. So, we've got to—the question—the strategic question is,

What if they don't stand up? Are we going to do it by ourselves? I think the answer has to be, we can't, not only because the American people aren't interested in it, but also because it isn't going to work. It has to—this war has to have a coalition face.

And the third strategic question, forgetting about this current battle, this is a battle in a long-term war. The real question, to me, is, What is our strategy for dealing with radical jihadism, generally, not just ISIL? I—you know, we've got al-Qaeda, ISIL, al-Shabaab, Boko Haram, AQAP, al-Nusra. This is geopolitical whack-a-mole, and we've got to have a strategy to get to the bottom of, Why are young people joining these organizations? What's motivating them? What—how do we counter their message that is attracting people into this radical death-oriented philosophy?

And so, I think I would urge the administration—you've got to deal with the current crisis, I understand that. And I think ISIL is a threat. But, we also have to deal with, okay, what happens if the Iraqi army can't—doesn't stand up adequately? And what happens if we're—our troops that we train in Syria are unable to really take the fight to ISIL?

The third question which I think is important is, we've got to have a longer term, more broad strategy to deal with this threat. Otherwise, this is going to be a 100-year war. And I just don't think it's in anyone's interest to contemplate such a terrible outcome.

Again, I want to thank you, gentlemen, and your testimony has been very helpful today, both of you.

Chairman LEVIN. Thank you, Senator King.

Senator Gillibrand.

Senator GILLIBRAND. Thank you, Mr. Chairman.

And thank you both for your service and being here today.

Secretary Hagel, much has been talked about the role of Turkey and concerns about foreign fighters using their territory to cross in to aid the fighting. When you were in Turkey last week, what can you tell us about our engagement with Turkey to help stream the tide of the foreign fighter flow? And also, Turkey really hasn't committed publicly to what it will do as part of the core coalition. What can you tell us about their intentions with regard to this effort?

Secretary HAGEL. Thank you, Senator. And I know, as you have expressed it, other Senators, the importance of Turkey, here. And we agree.

First, you know that ISIL is currently holding 46 Turkish diplomats hostage. In my conversations with President Erdogan and the new Prime Minister, Davutoglu, all their senior leaders, this obviously was at the top of their priority list, which it would be. Secretary Kerry was there a few days after I was there.

Now, that said, Turkey recognizes, as much as any country, the threat that ISIL poses as other extremist groups. They are working with us now, will continue to work with us. Obviously, in an open hearing, I have to be careful that—I can't go too far down into this. We'd be glad to, in a closed session, give you more. But, the——

Senator GILLIBRAND. And also, the oil on the black market. Because——

Secretary HAGEL. That's another issue that——

Senator GILLIBRAND.—it's a huge financing stream for them.

Secretary HAGEL.—it's another issue that we talk to them about. They're not unaware of that. They know that it's a threat. They know that it's a major funding source of ISIL. They are moving to deal with the—some of these same issues. Our interests are common and clear. I think it's important to recognize, again, that Turkey has been an invaluable member of NATO, still is. We have a NATO base there. We have a lot going on with Turkey, as do other NATO countries. So, their interests are clear, and they understand that in this fight.

Senator GILLIBRAND. Many of the members of this committee have talked about the effectiveness of arming the moderate rebels. Senator Hirono just had a line of questioning about, What agreements do they have with them? The Sotloff family have made certain questions about what information the moderates may have given to ISIL about their son. So, I'm concerned about how we assess their abilities, their effectiveness, how we can—you know, when I met some of these opposition fighters in—the last time I was overseas, they wouldn't even agree to locking down and securing chemical weapons, when they were found, and turning them over to an international body. And so, how can you engage them? How can you truly vet them? And how can we have any hope that, if they do agree to fight ISIL on some level, not just Assad, that they will continue to do so and not align themselves with ISIL when they feel like Assad is in their sights?

Secretary HAGEL. I think a couple of points need to be reemphasized to answer your question. And General Dempsey has talked about it today. I have. In both our testimonies. First, it goes back to a couple of recent questions that were asked here in the last few minutes. The United States cannot do any of this alone. This is why the local people—the local efforts, local organization has to be involved in this.

Second, confidence and trust in their governments. When you really look at—with some intensity here, what's going on in Syria, how did this happen, why was it allowed to happen in Iraq, how did the Sunni tribes just walk away from the government, three divisions of the Iraqi Security Forces dropping their weapons and running—why did all that happen? Well, General Dempsey—I know it's complicated, but he made a very important point. When people are disenfranchised, they don't trust their government, they don't have confidence in their government, their will to fight and to do the things that you're talking about won't be there. So, to reestablish trust and confidence coming from the locals, helping the locals—helping sustain them, build them, development—is really the—I think, is much the answer to the question as anyone thinks.

Senator GILLIBRAND. But, the moderate fighters, specifically, their goals are to unseat Assad. That is their primary reason for fighting. So, if we add this additional mission to them, "We are going to help you, but you must help defeat ISIL," I don't know what makes them trade off one mission for the other. I don't know what hook you have that says, "You have to help us defeat ISIL, and we'll assist in this" in a way that they don't, at some point, say, "No, our goal is to defeat Assad, and the way to defeat Assad is give all the weapons you just gave us to these better fighters that are represented by ISIL."

Secretary HAGEL. I don't think they see it as an either/or. ISIL is a clear threat to them. What ISIL has done to them, to their people, their families, decimated their villages, the atrocities that ISIL has perpetrated on these people in Syria—so, it isn't a matter of, "We'll fight either ISIL or Assad."

What I believe—and I think we have pretty clear intelligence on this, and just—the responsibility that we all have of understanding the people, first, is—it's pretty clear they want a future for their families, they want to live in some peace and stability, with possibilities for their families—jobs. One of the points that was made here earlier this morning—and I think General Dempsey made it—until there's some clarification on these millions of disenfranchised young men in North Africa, the Middle East, with no jobs, no possibilities, nothing, no hope, despair, then one country isn't going to be able to fix this problem. This is a deep, wide problem. And I think it really does reflect back on your question.

So, we can't do it alone. It is a long-term effort. But, the threats to us are so clear now, and to these people, that we have to deal with it.

Senator GILLIBRAND. Thank you.

Chairman LEVIN. Thank you.

I just want to clarify one number I think you both have used, a 5,000 goal for the DOD train-and-equip program. If—and this is an "if"—as reported—as published reports indicate, there's a covert program—I'm saying "if"—any numbers involved in that covert program would not be involved in the 5,000. Is that correct?

General DEMPSEY. That's correct.

Chairman LEVIN. Thank you.

We thank you very much for being here, for your testimony.

We stand adjourned.

[Whereupon, at 1:09 p.m., the committee adjourned.]